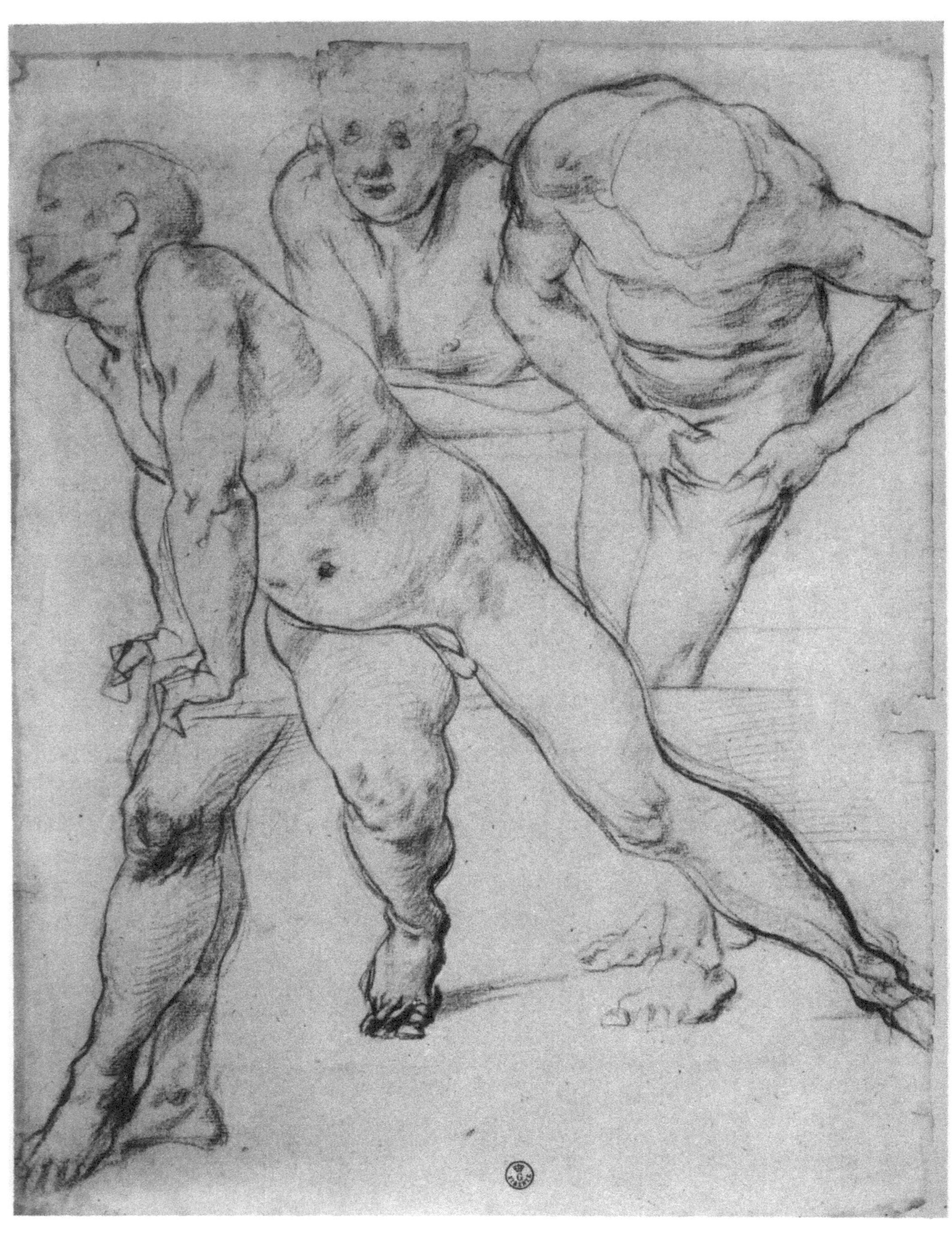

Jacopo Pontormo (1494–1556/57). Study of a nude in various positions. Sanguine; 378 × 288 mm. Louvre, Paris.

OLD MASTER LIFE DRAWINGS

44 Plates

Edited by James Spero

Dover Publications, Inc., New York

PUBLISHER'S NOTE

The depiction of the human nude is perhaps the most difficult challenge facing an artist. To represent successfully a nude figure on a planar surface, he must possess the technical abilities to create mass and form through line, to cope with proportion and foreshortening, and to handle media such as crayon, charcoal, ink and wash. The artist must also have an understanding of anatomy profound enough to allow him to take certain liberties that nevertheless do not prevent the work from remaining persuasive and true.

Taken from various rare portfolios, this anthology reproduces works by masters ranging from Filippino Lippi to Ingres to show different approaches to life drawing. With a precise, lively line, Raphael (p. 19) plays contour against masses indicated by hatching; Michelangelo's meticulous shading (p. 12) produces an undulating surface reminiscent of one of his statues; the virtuosity of Titian's bold composition (p. 41) suggests a more painterly viewpoint.

These works also reveal two fundamental concepts of the nude: the heroic tradition emphasizing the perfection of the human body (for example, the study by Rosso Fiorentino, p. 22) that stands in contrast to the approach that depicts the body as frail and mortal (as in the Rembrandt drawing, p. 20).

The captions list artist, years of birth and death, subject, medium, dimensions (in millimeters, height before width) and location. Full information was unavailable for some drawings.

Old Master Life Drawings: 44 Plates is a new work, first published by Dover Publications, Inc., in 1986.

Library of Congress Cataloging-in-Publication Data

Old master life drawings.

   1. Figure drawing—catalogs. 2. Nude in art—Catalogs. I. Spero, James.
NC765.05 1986   741.94'074   86-19294
ISBN-13: 978-0-486-25233-9 (pbk.)
ISBN-10: 0-486-25233-7 (pbk.)

Manufactured in the United States by LSC Communications
25233714   2018
www.doverpublications.com

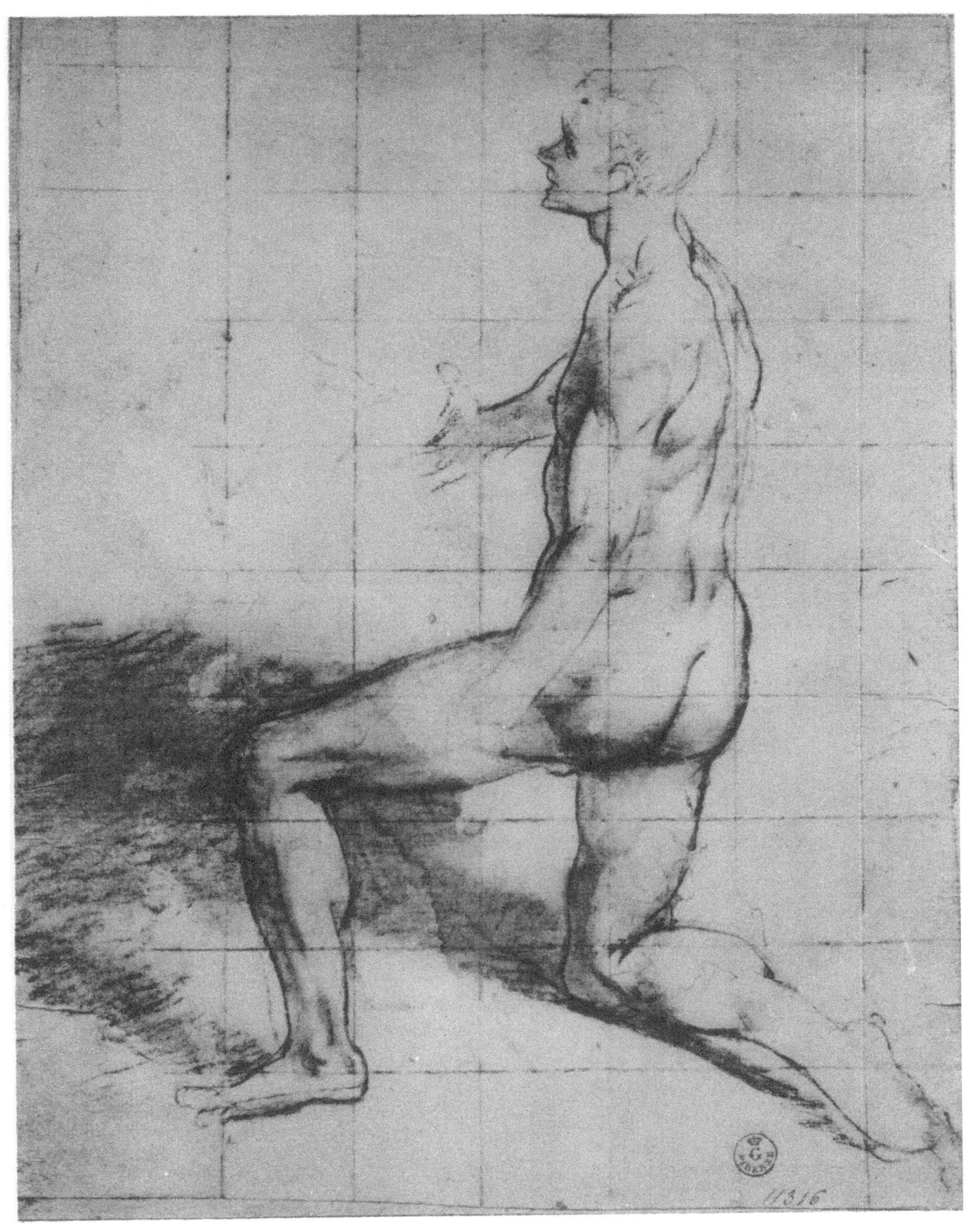

Federigo Baroccio (or Barocci; 1526–1612). Study for Saint Andrew. Chalk and charcoal;
350 × 274 mm. Uffizi Gallery, Florence.

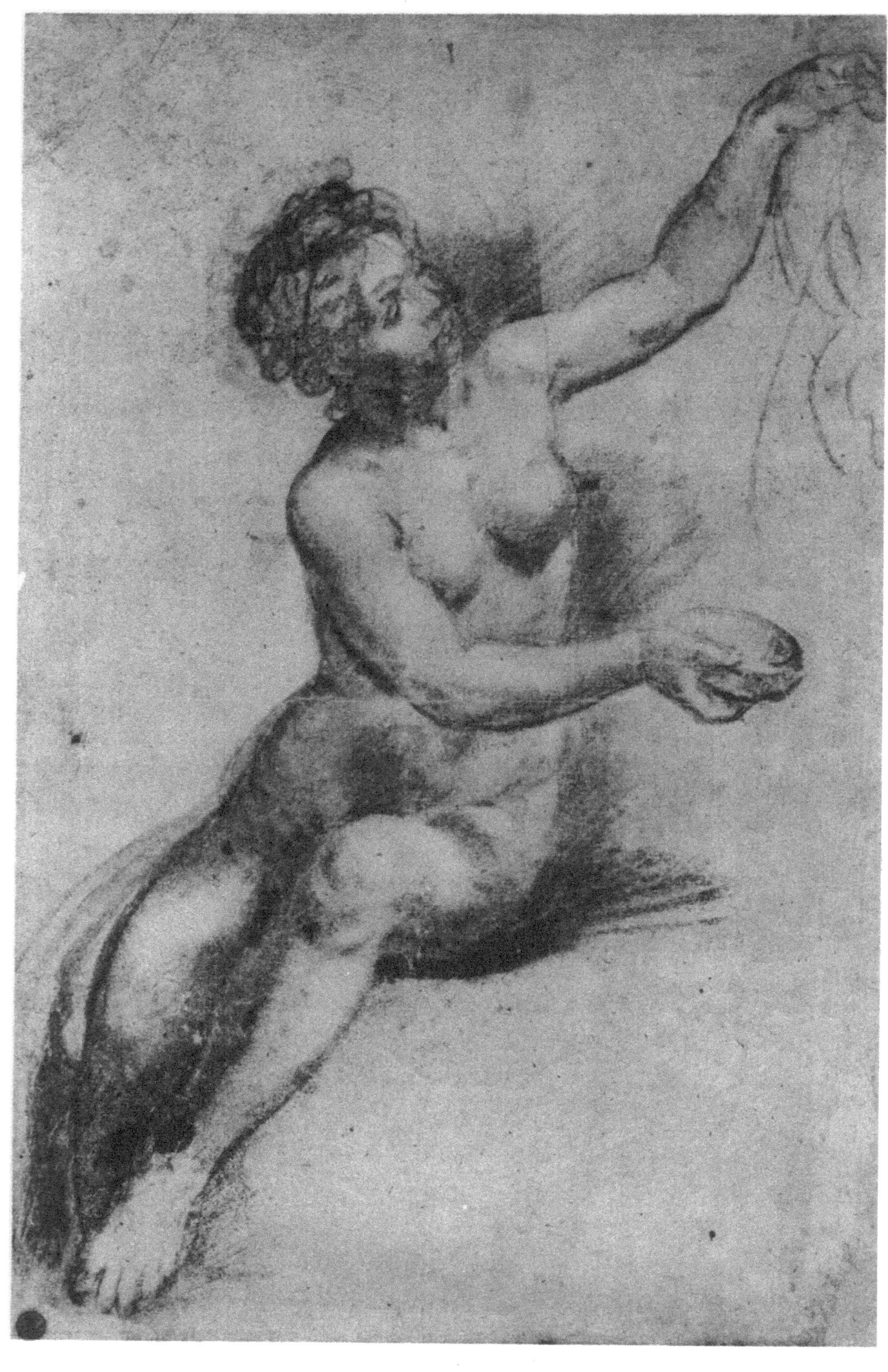

Paris Bordone (1500–1571). Female nude. Charcoal and chalk on cerulean paper; 200 × 320 mm. Uffizi Gallery, Florence.

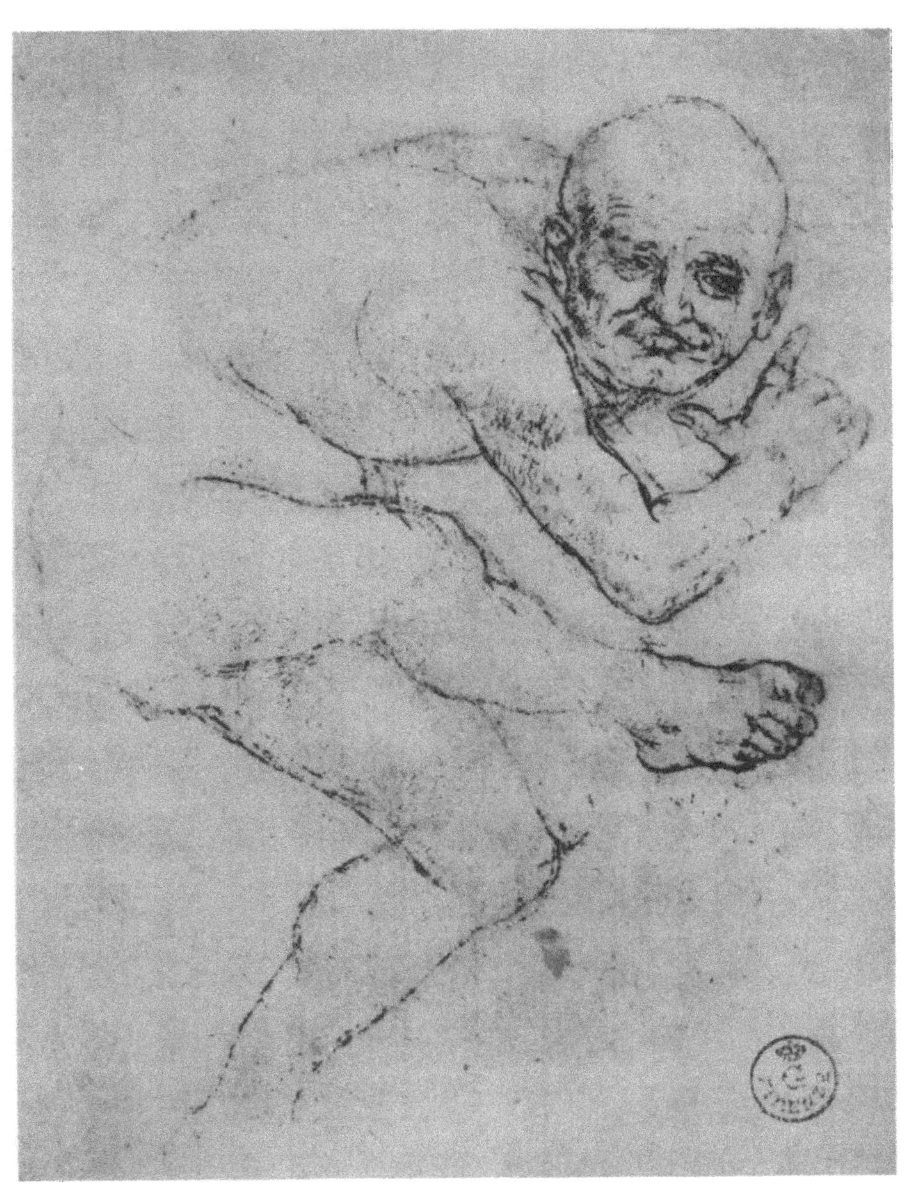

Pieter Brueghel the Elder? (ca. 1525–1569). Old man dancing. Pen and ink on white paper; 160 × 120 mm. Uffizi Gallery, Florence.

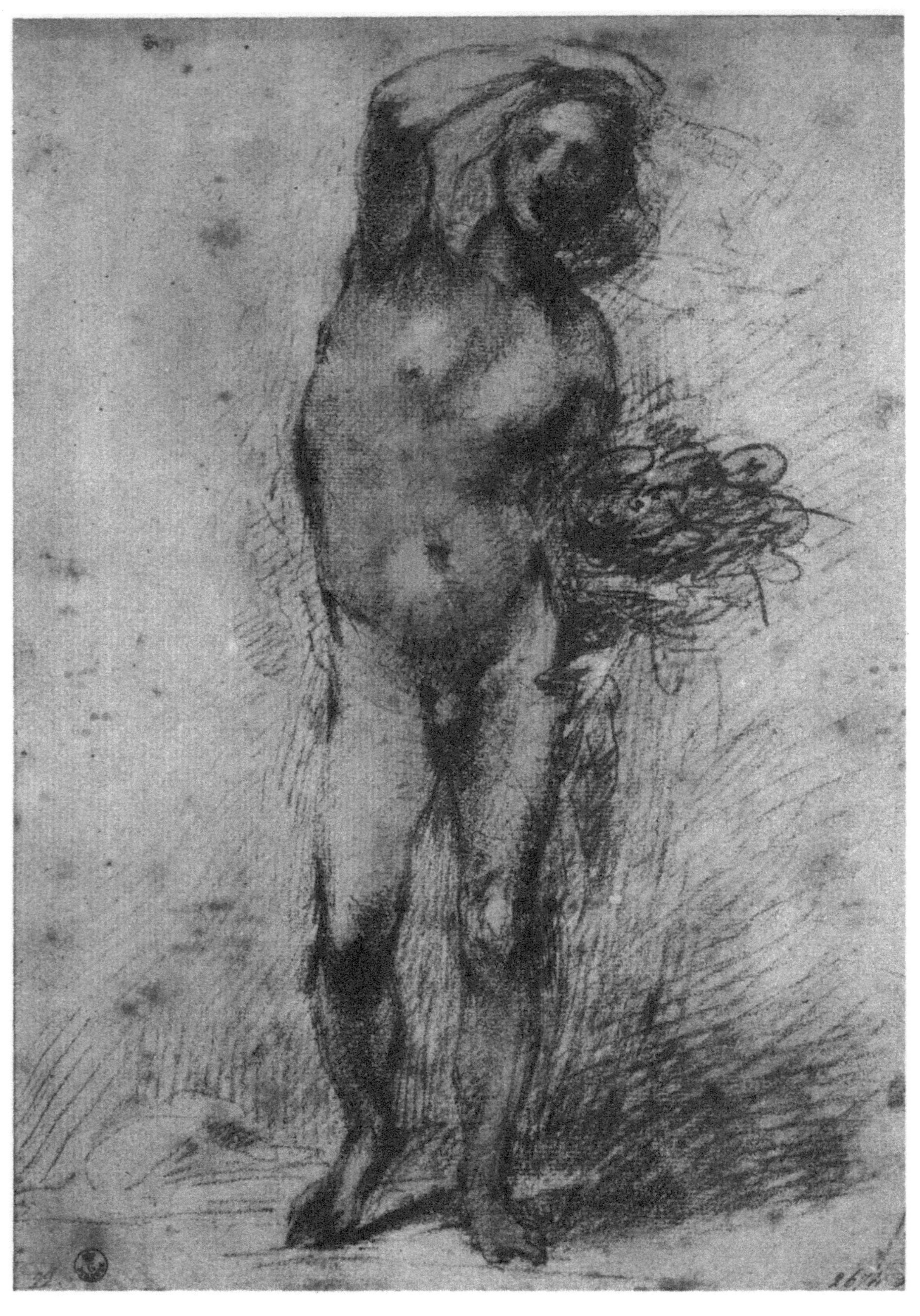

Cecco Bravo (Francesco Montelatici; ca. 1600–1661). Study of a nude youth. Sanguine and black chalk on white paper; 333 x 230 mm. Uffizi Gallery, Florence.

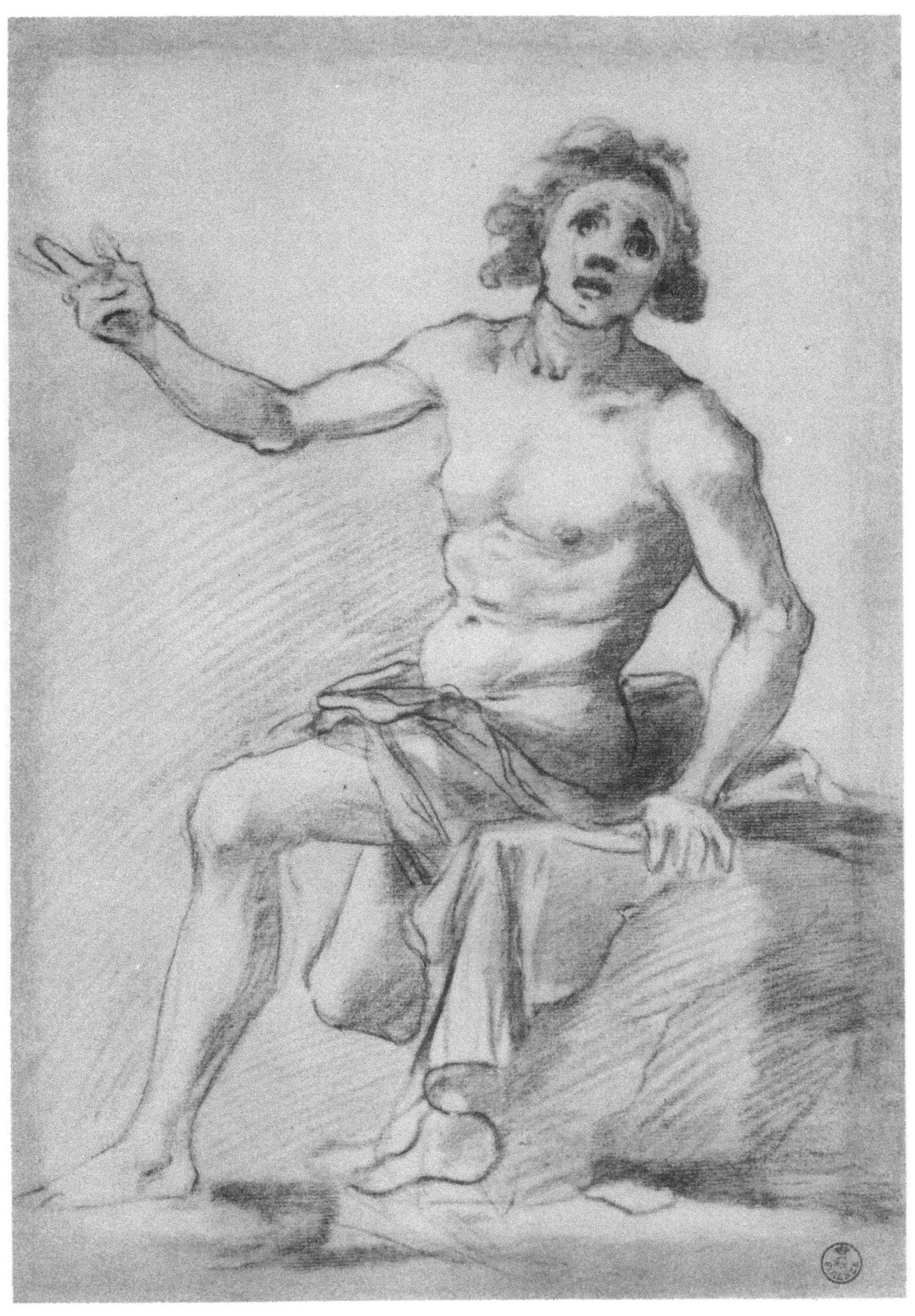

Jacopo da Empoli (Jacopo Chimenti; 1554–1640). Seminude male figure. Sanguine on white paper; 400 x 240 mm. Uffizi Gallery, Florence.

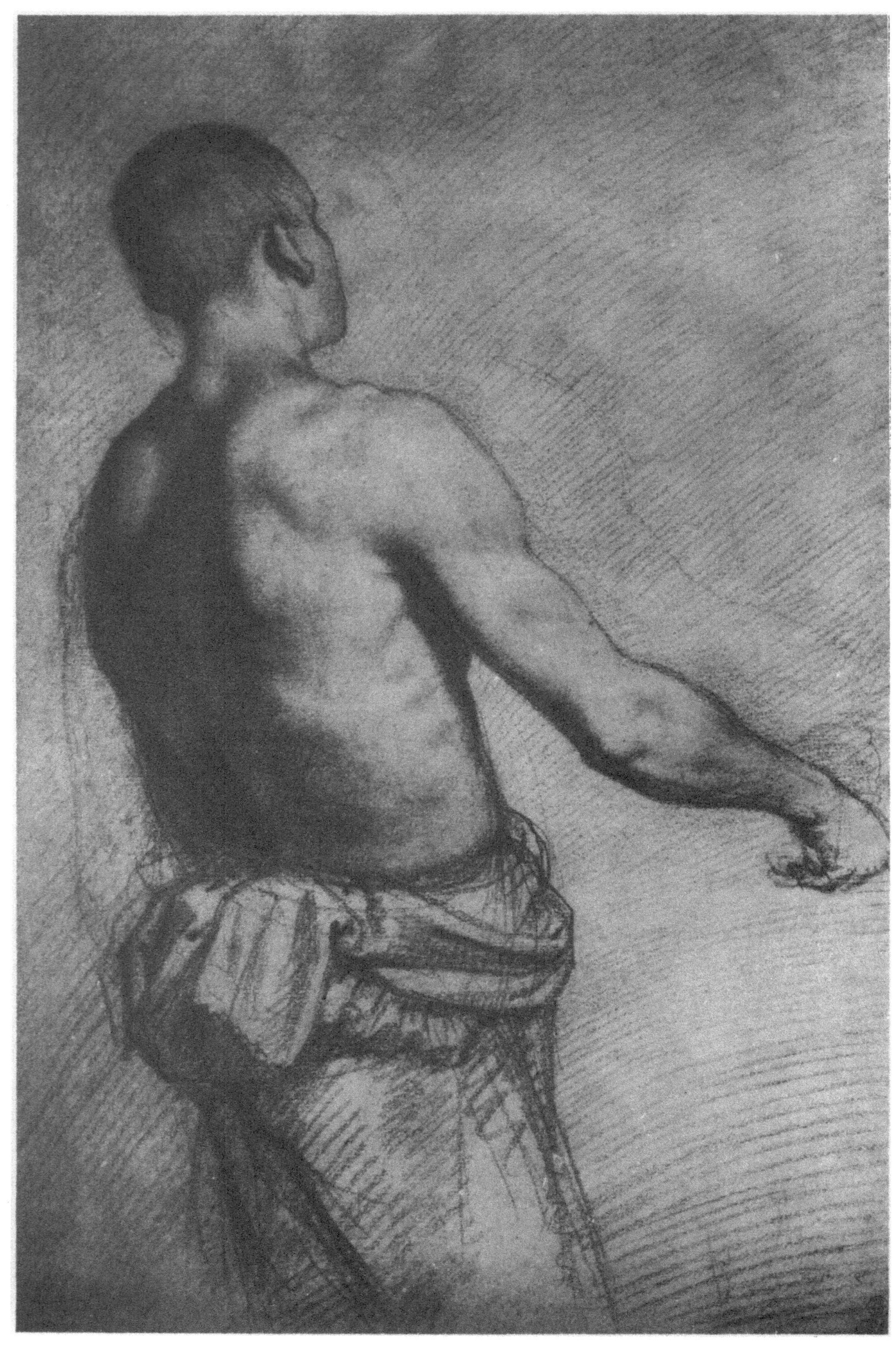

Jacopo da Empoli. Study of a youth naked to the waist. Sanguine. Pierpont Morgan Library, New York.

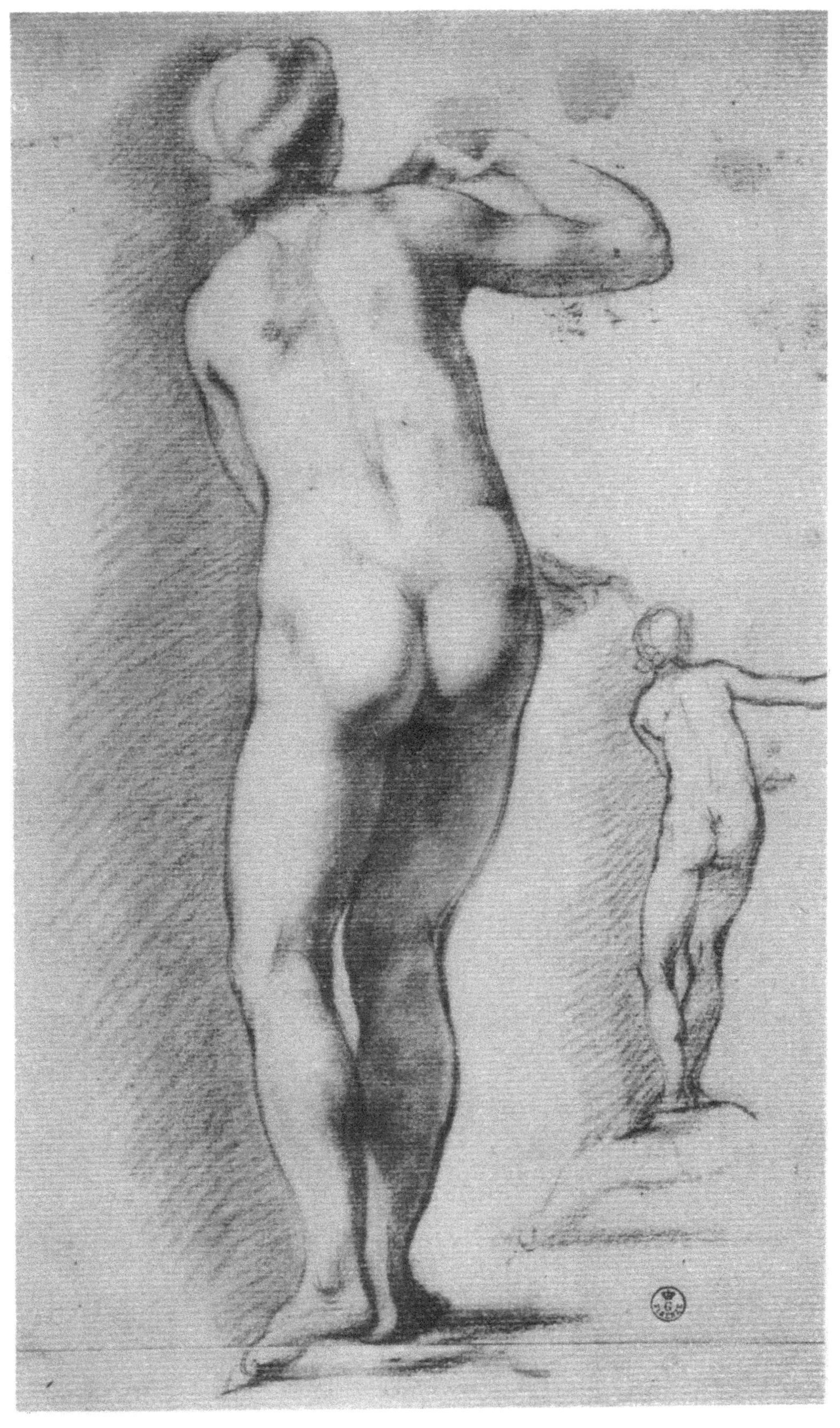

Francesco Furini (1604–1646). Female nude seen from the rear. Sanguine on white paper; 350 × 200 mm. Uffizi Gallery, Florence.

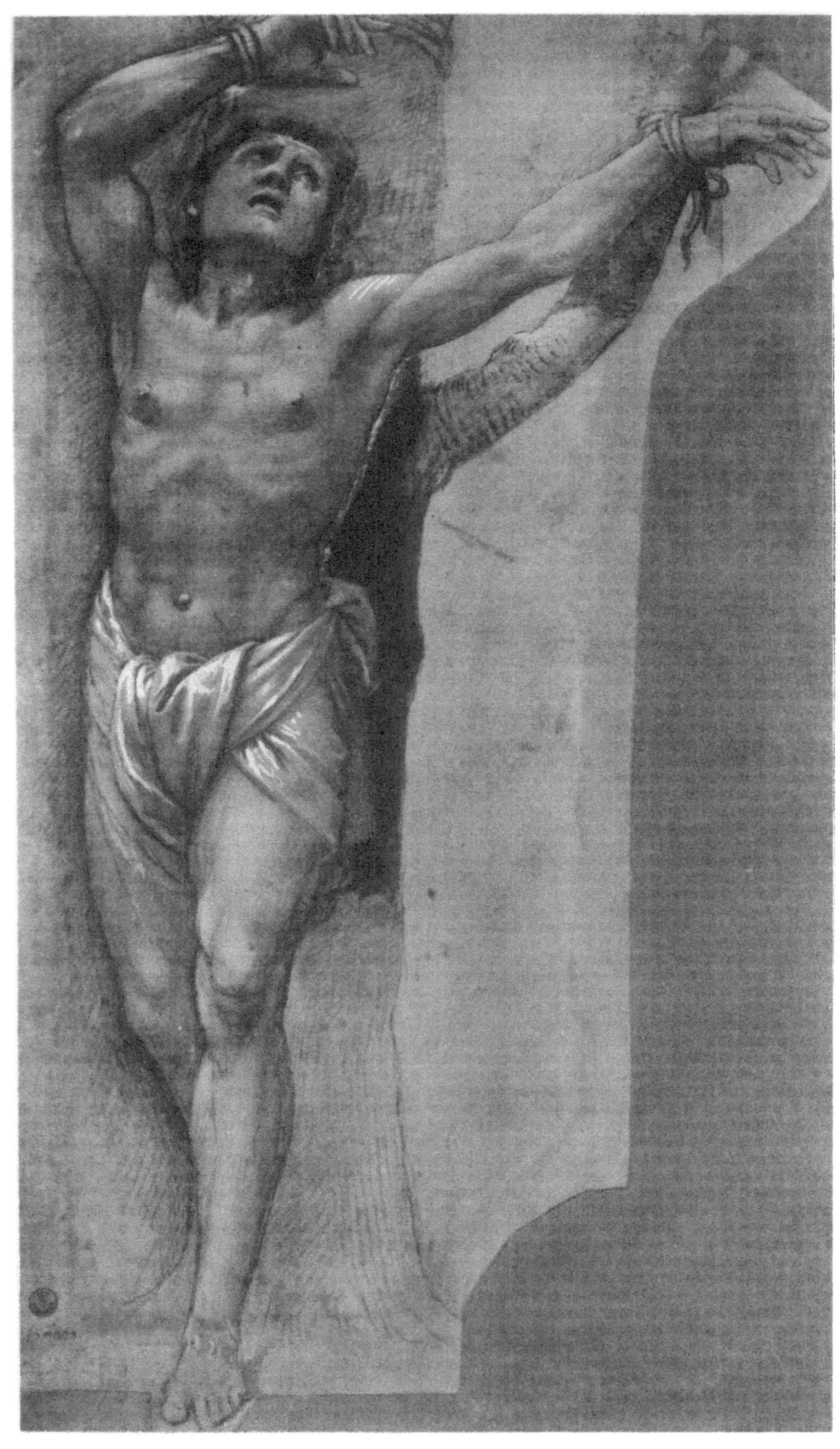

Gervasio Gatti (Il Sojaro; 1549–1631). Study for Saint Sebastian. Pencil and pen with lead heightening on cerulean paper; 240 × 430 mm. Uffizi Gallery, Florence.

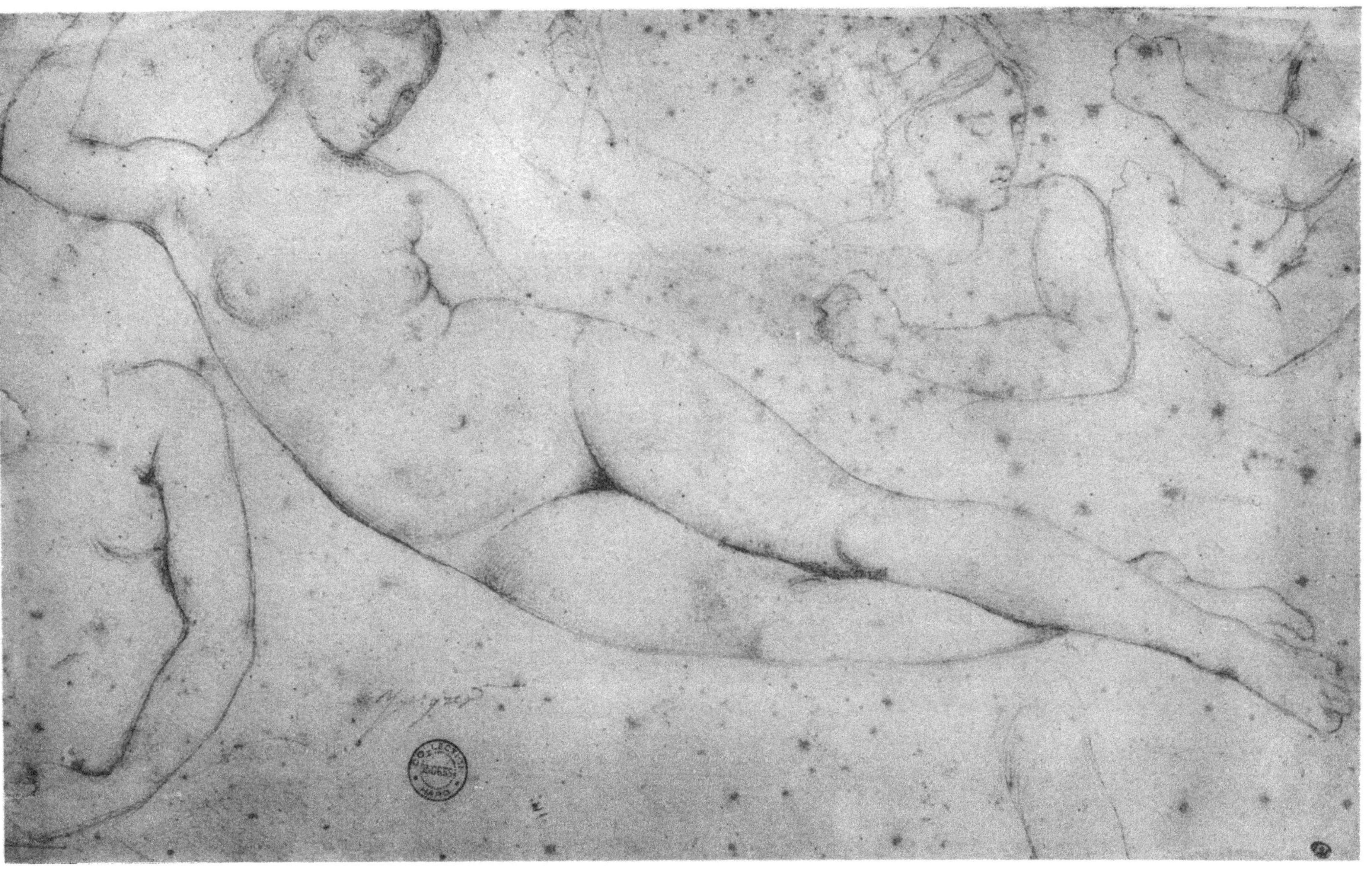

Jean-Auguste-Dominique Ingres (1780–1867). Study of a reclining female. Graphite. Library, École des Beaux-Arts, Paris.

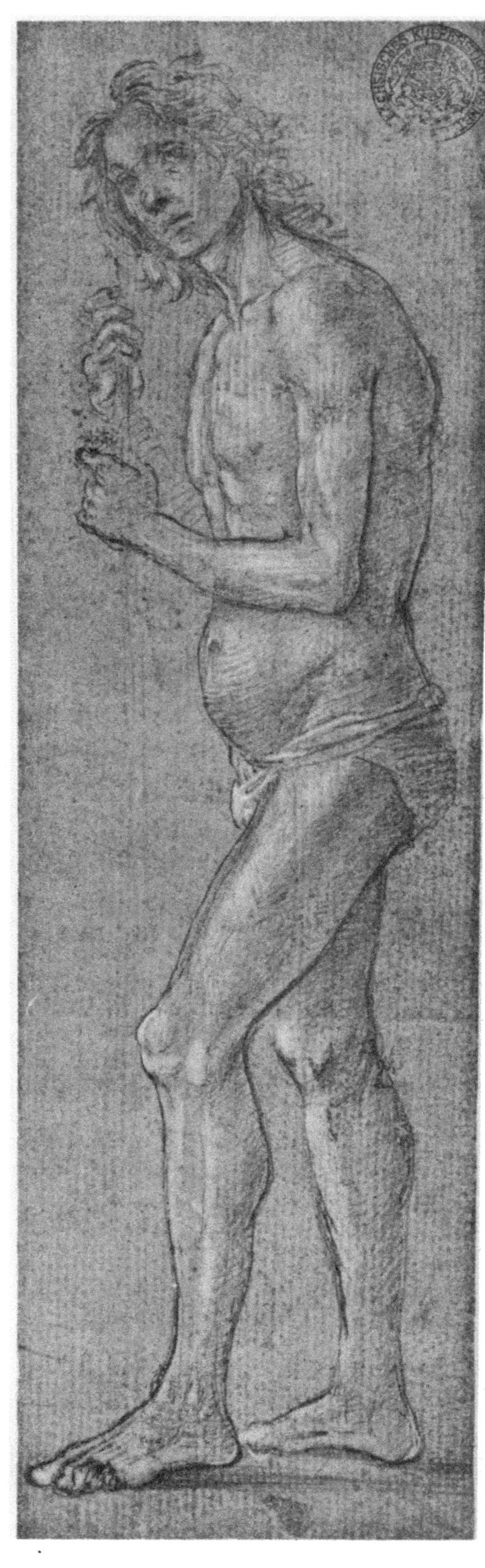

Filippino Lippi (1457–1504). A nude with staff, walking. Silverpoint heightened with white on grayish paper; 275 × 85 mm. Print Room, Dresden.

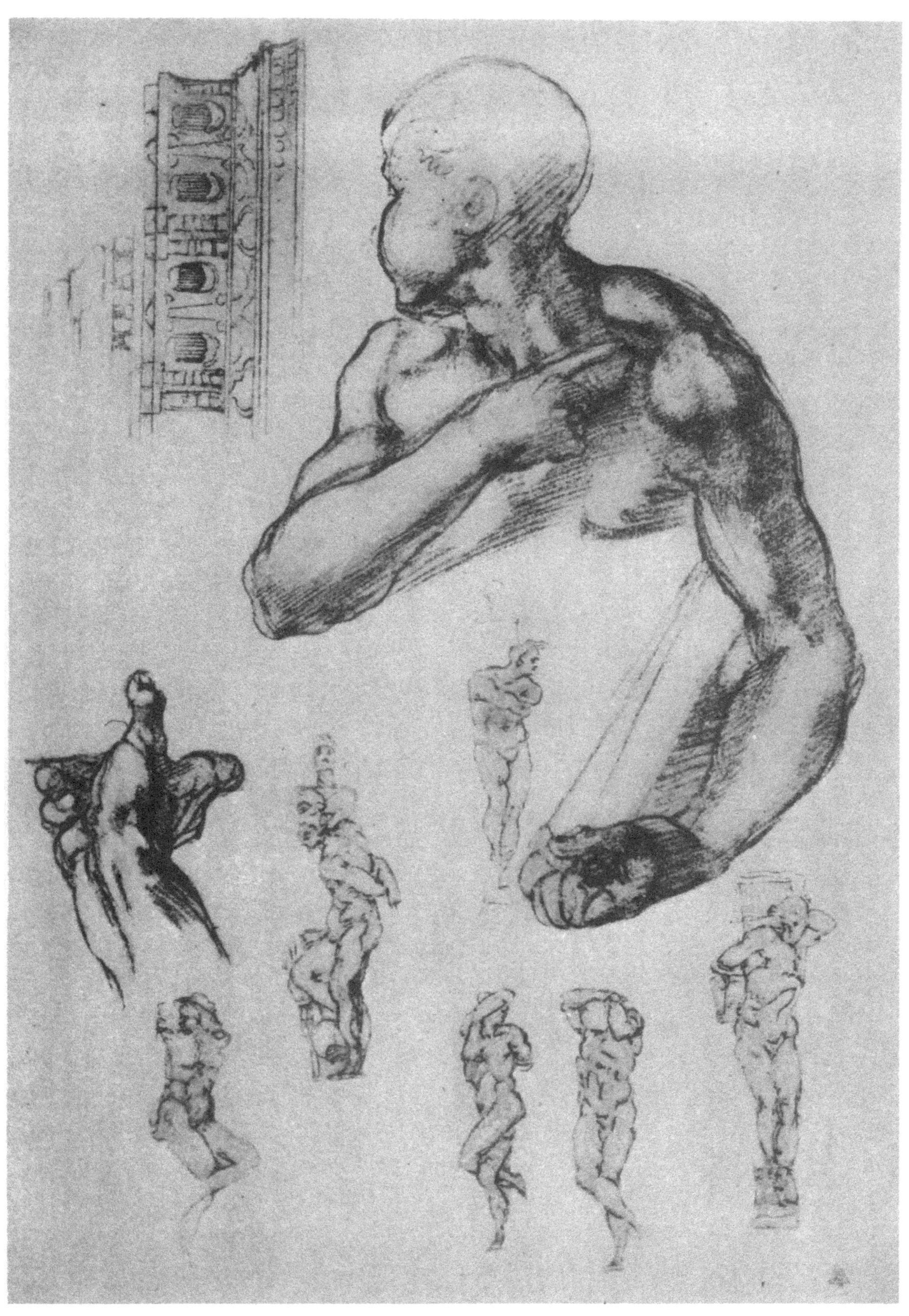

Michelangelo (Buonarroti; 1475–1564). Studies for: a figure and the right hand of the
Libyan Sibyl for the Sistine Chapel; six bound slaves for the tomb of Julius II; a cornice.
Sanguine; 285 × 195 mm. Oxford University Galleries, Oxford.

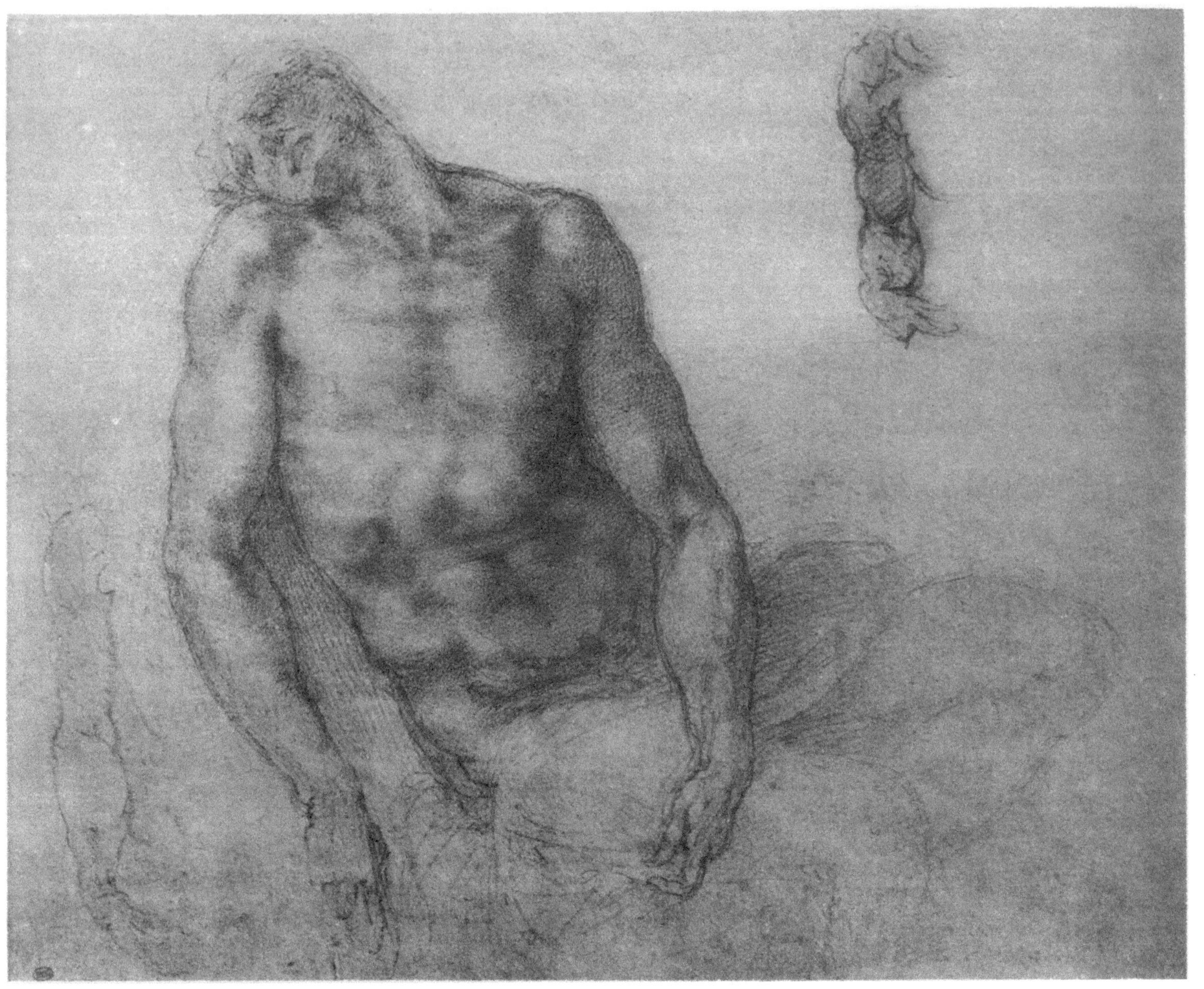

Michelangelo. Study for a dead Christ. Black chalk; 225 × 320 mm. Louvre, Paris.

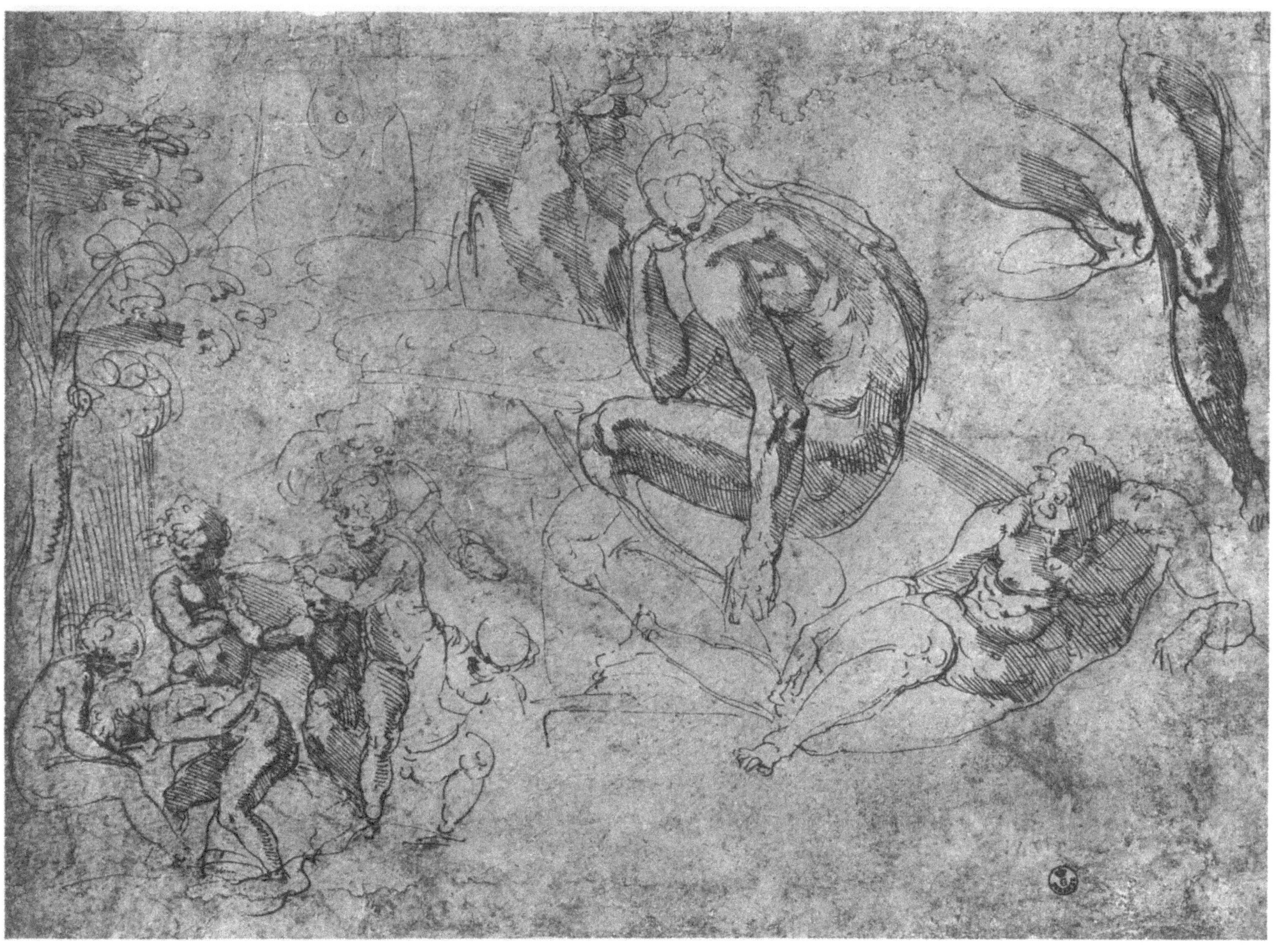

Raffaele de Montelupo (Sinibaldi; 1505?–1556). Children playing at hot cockles; two nudes. Pen and ink; 275 x 370 mm. Uffizi Gallery, Florence.

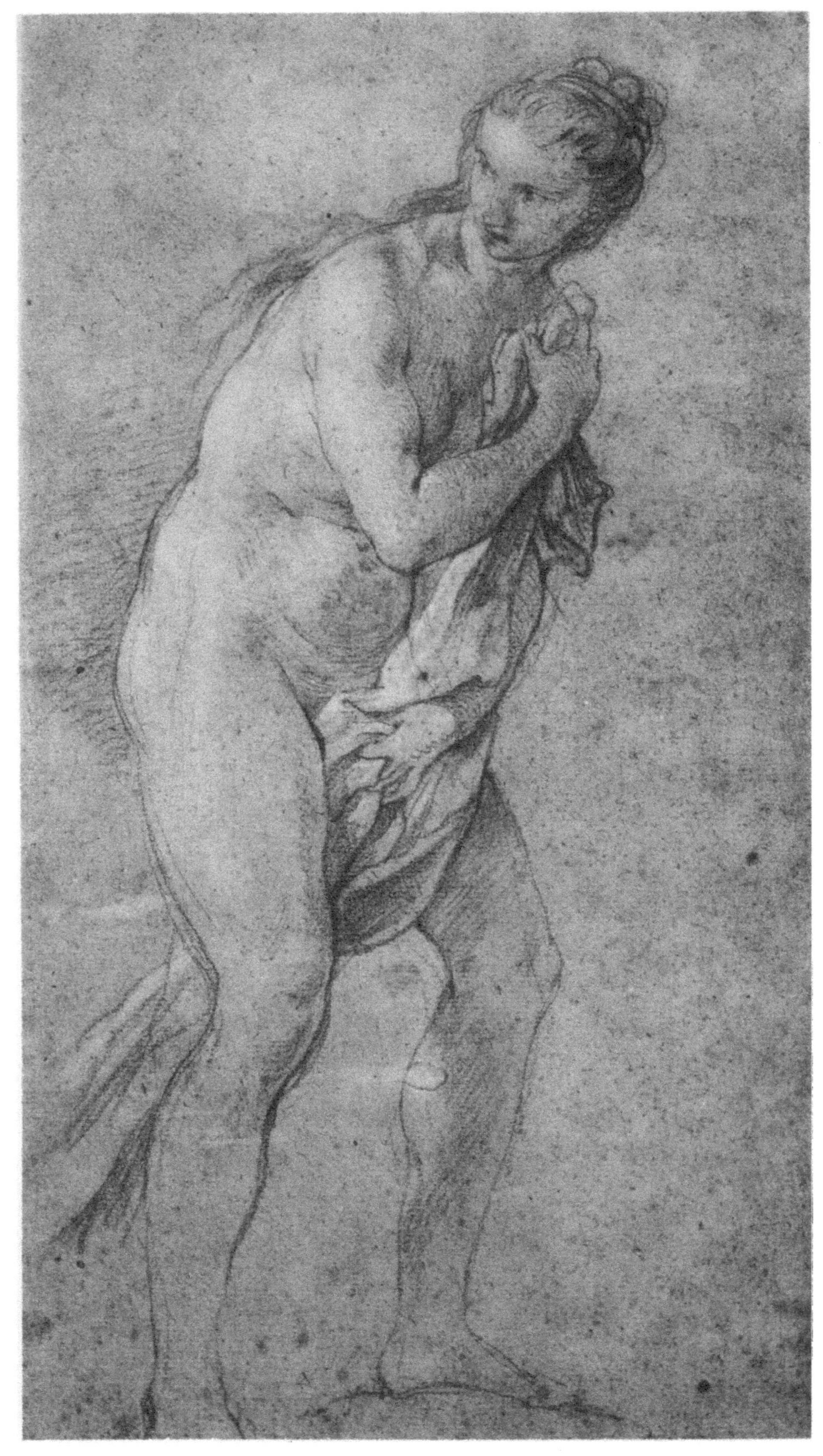

Charles Natoire (1700–1777). Surprised nymph. Sanguine on brownish-gray paper; 382 × 207 mm.

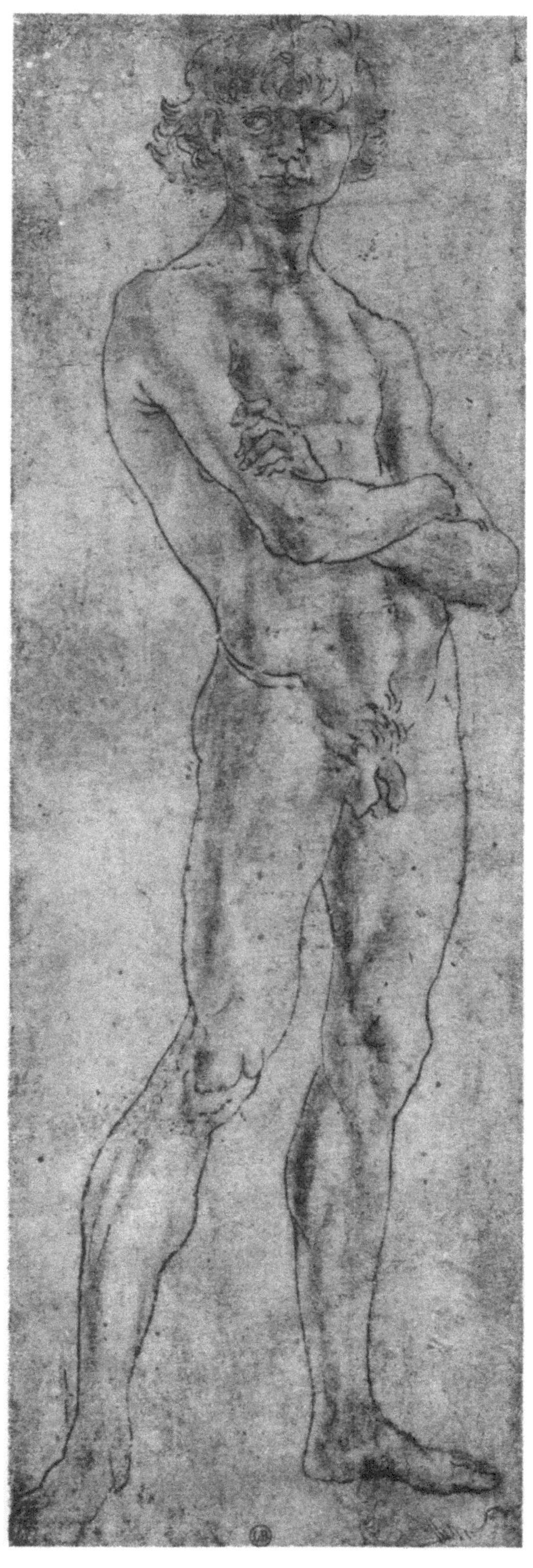

School of Pollaiuolo. A nude with folded arms. Pen and bister; 260 × 80 mm.

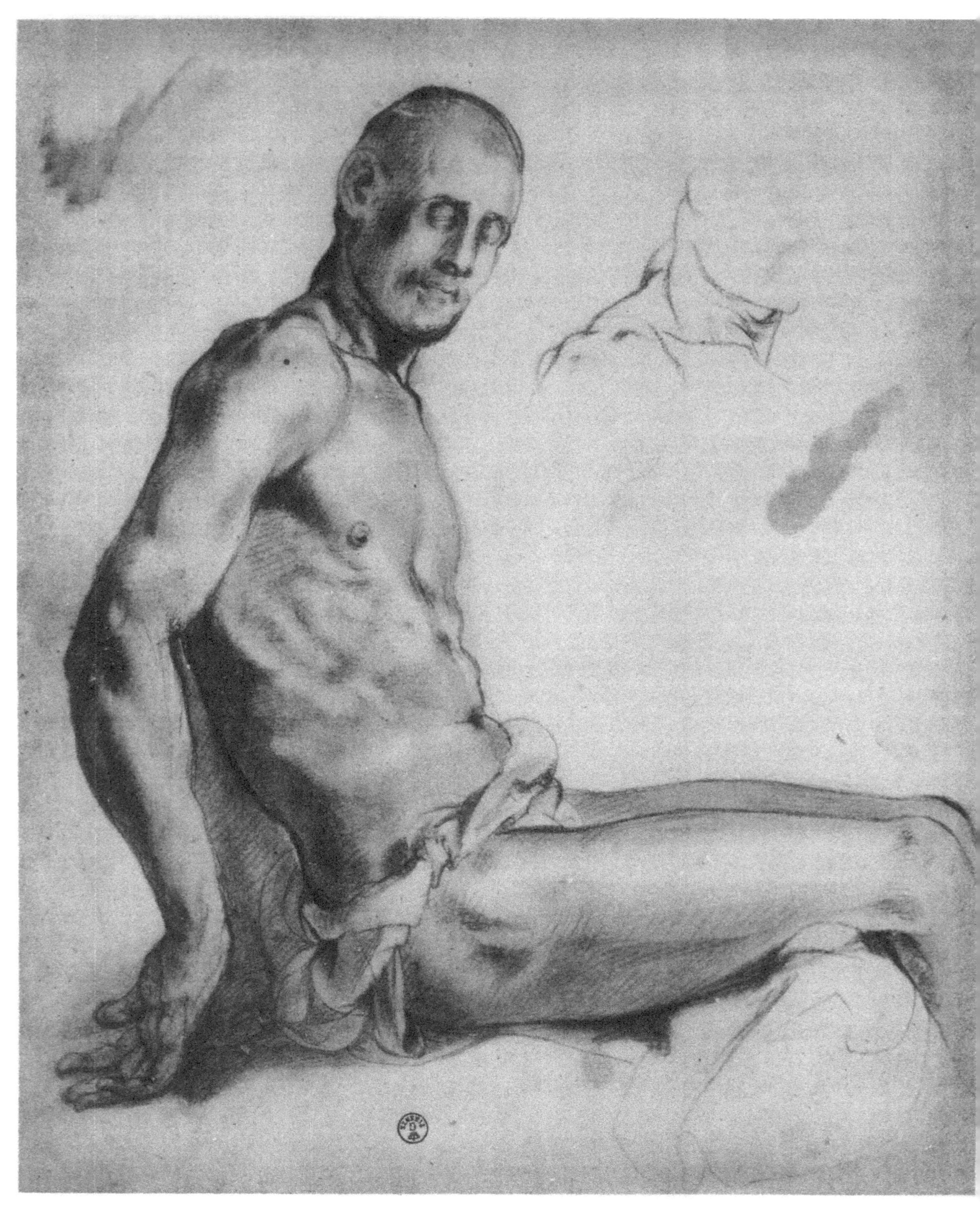

Jacopo Pontormo. Study for a dead Christ. Sanguine; 353 × 279 mm. Uffizi Gallery, Florence.

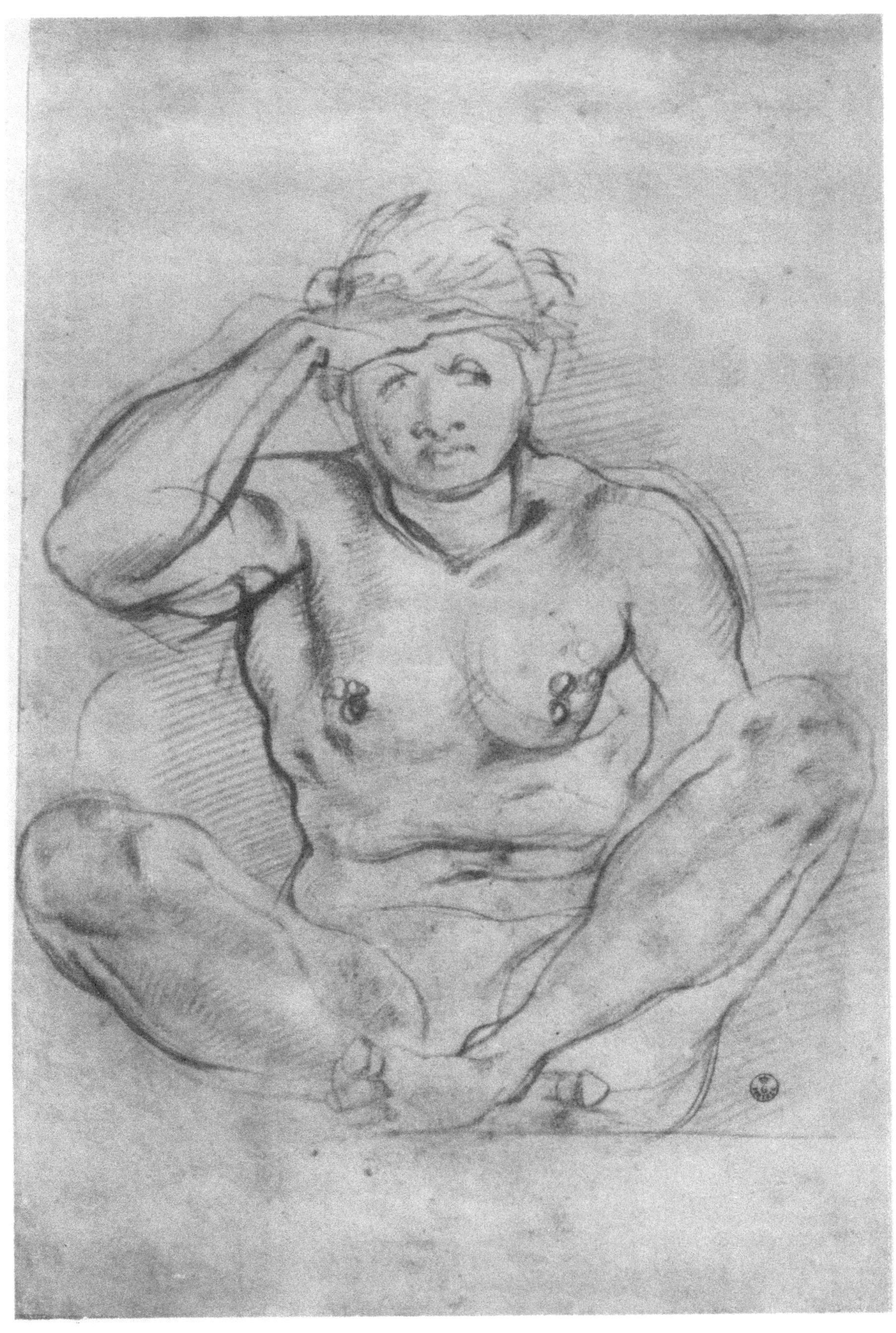

Jacopo Pontormo. Study of a nude seated on the ground. Black chalk; 400 × 260 mm.
Uffizi Gallery, Florence.

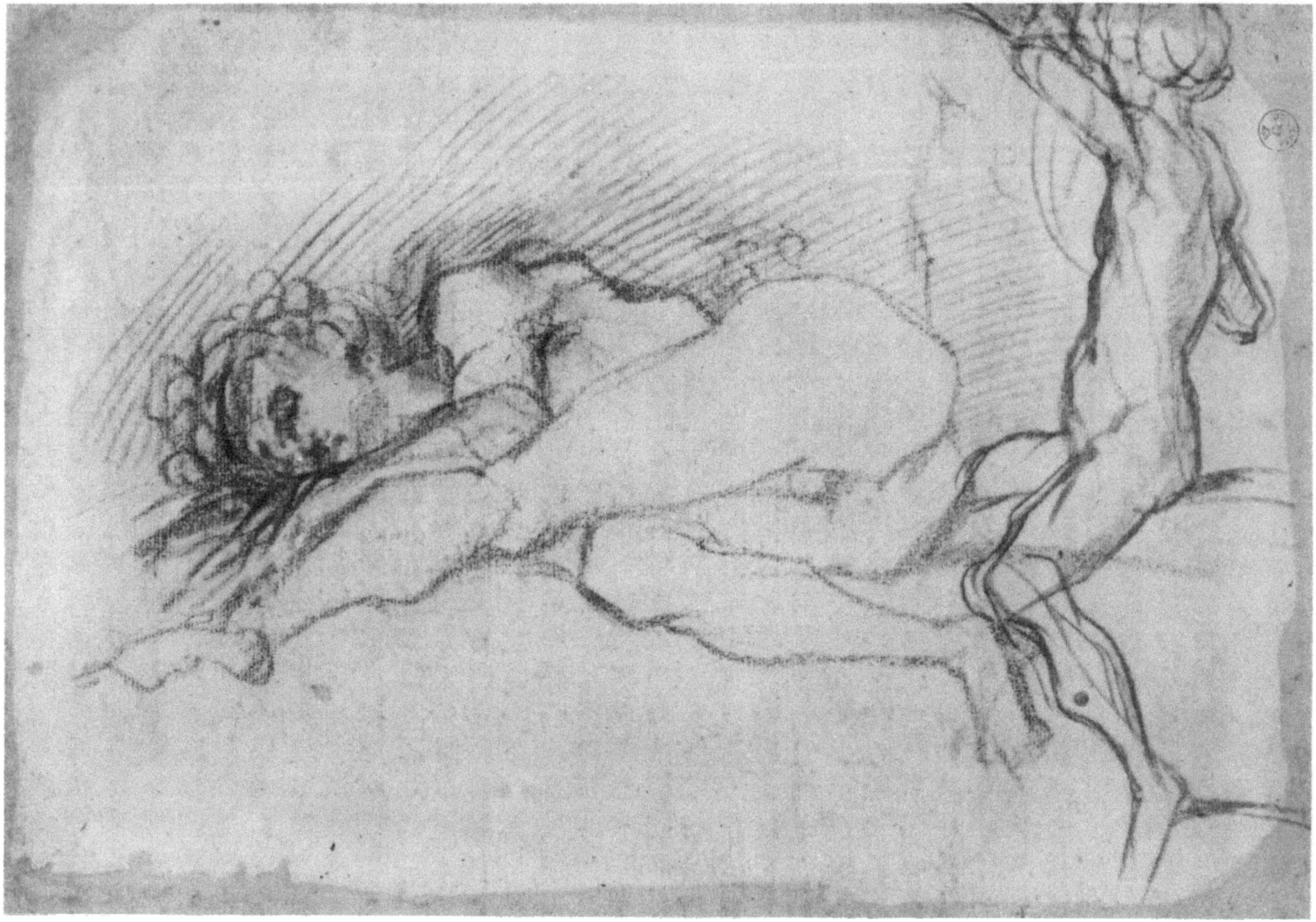

Jacopo Pontormo. Recumbent figure, foreshortened; a seated child. Black chalk; 400 × 280 mm. Uffizi Gallery, Florence.

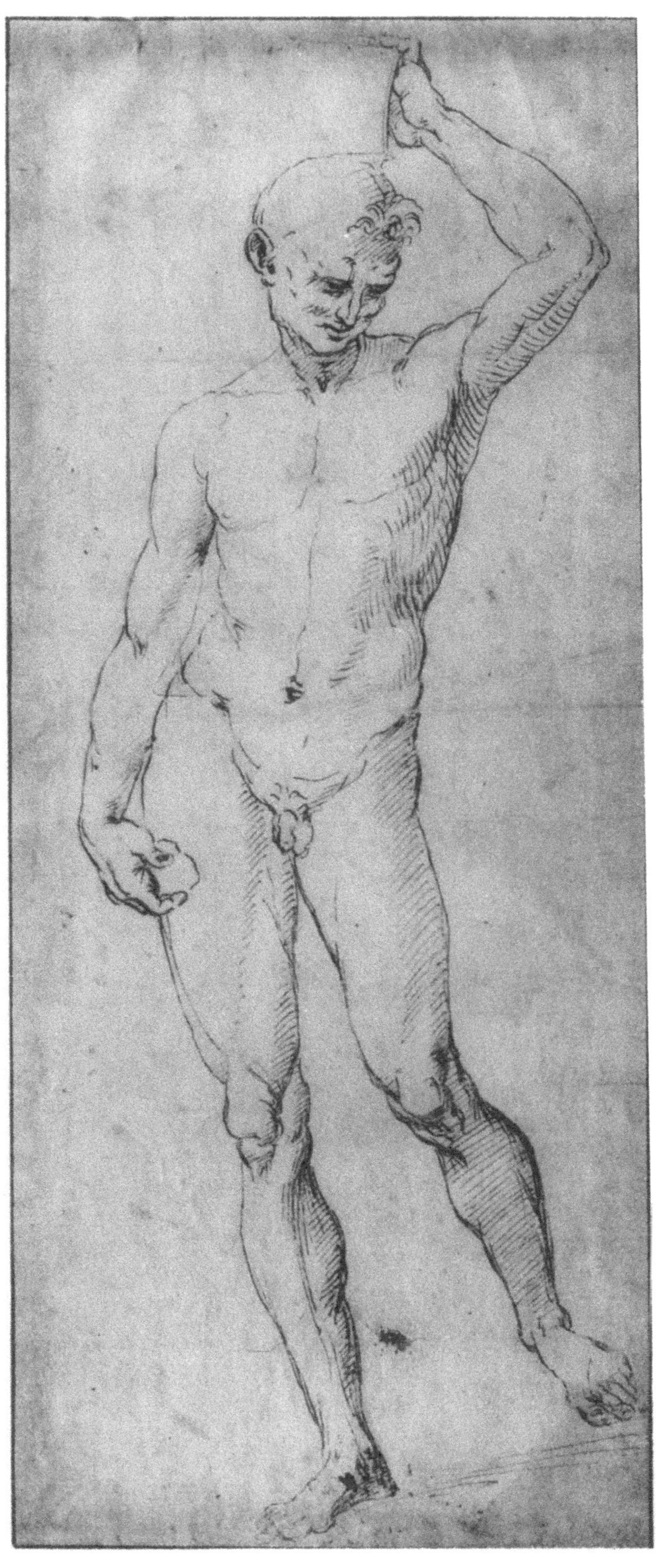

Raphael (Raffaello Sanzio; 1483–1520). Nude study of a man holding a vase on his head. Pen and bister.

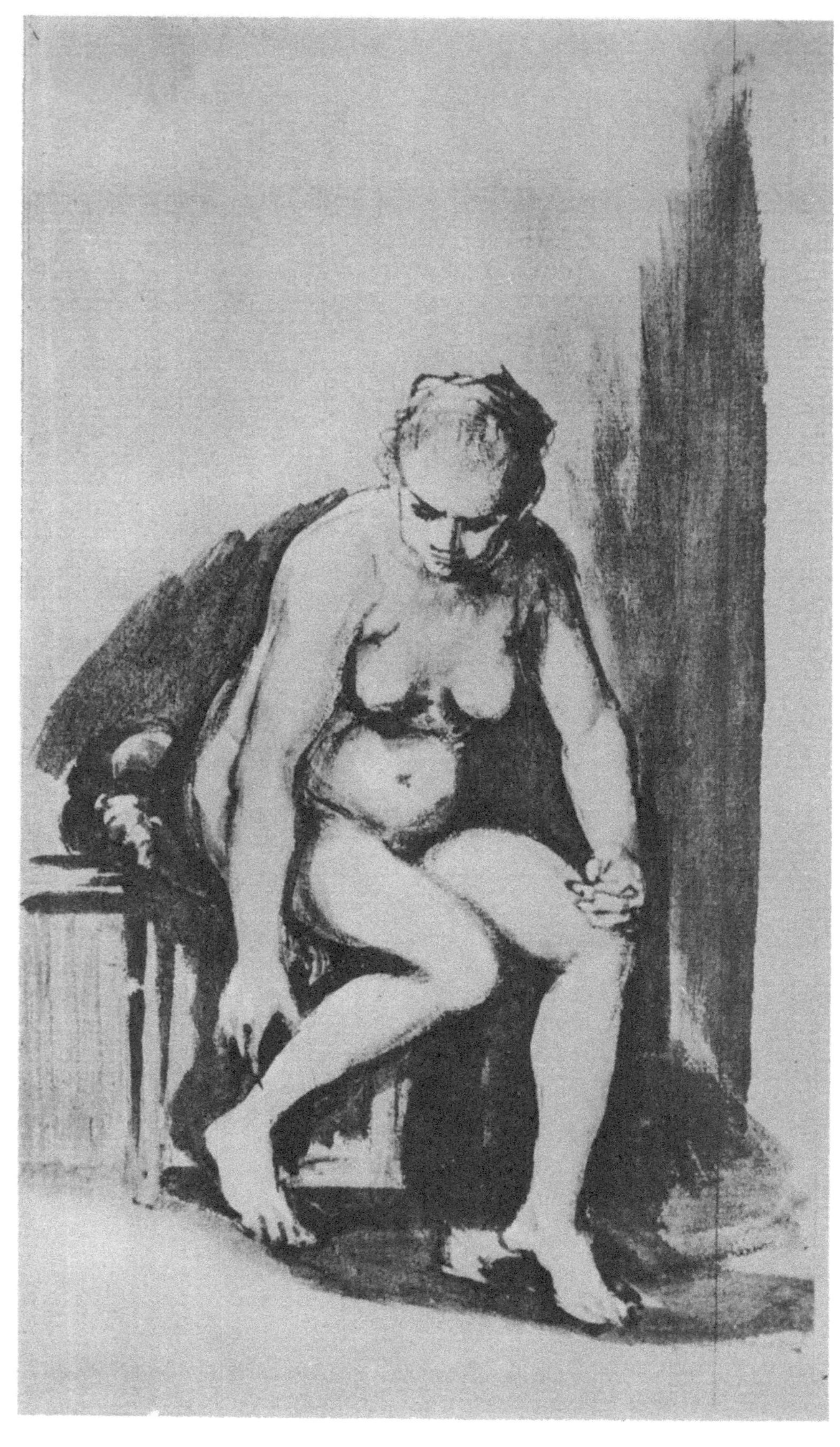

Rembrandt (Harmenszoon van Rijn; 1606–1669). Seated woman. British Museum, London.

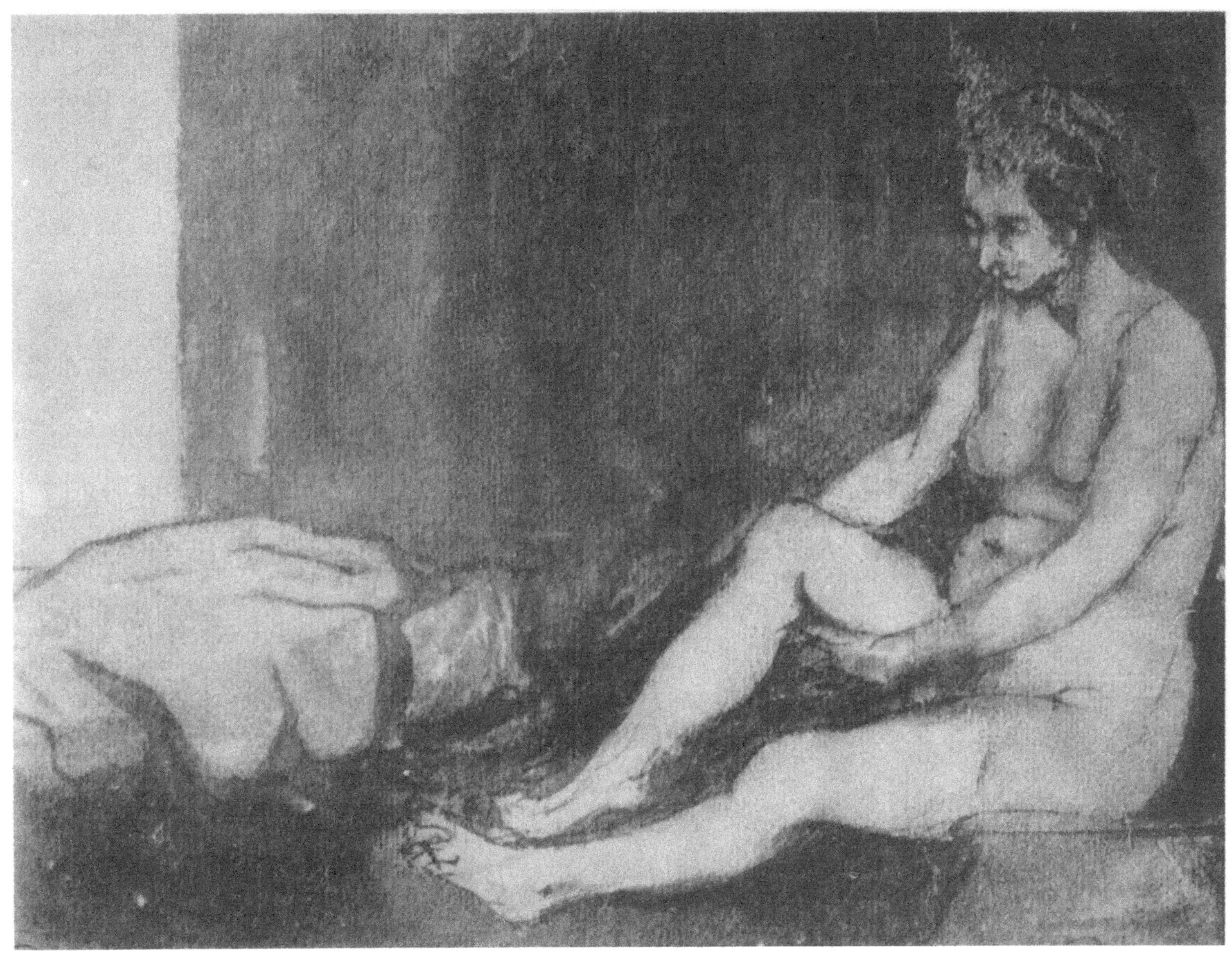

Rembrandt. Seated woman. Louvre, Paris.

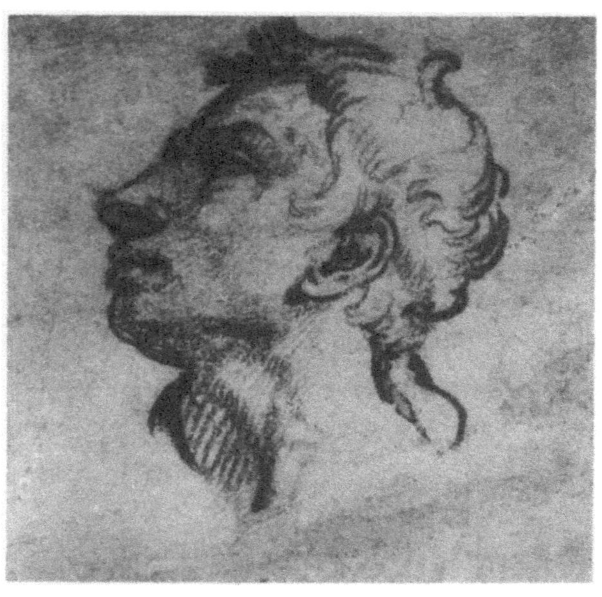

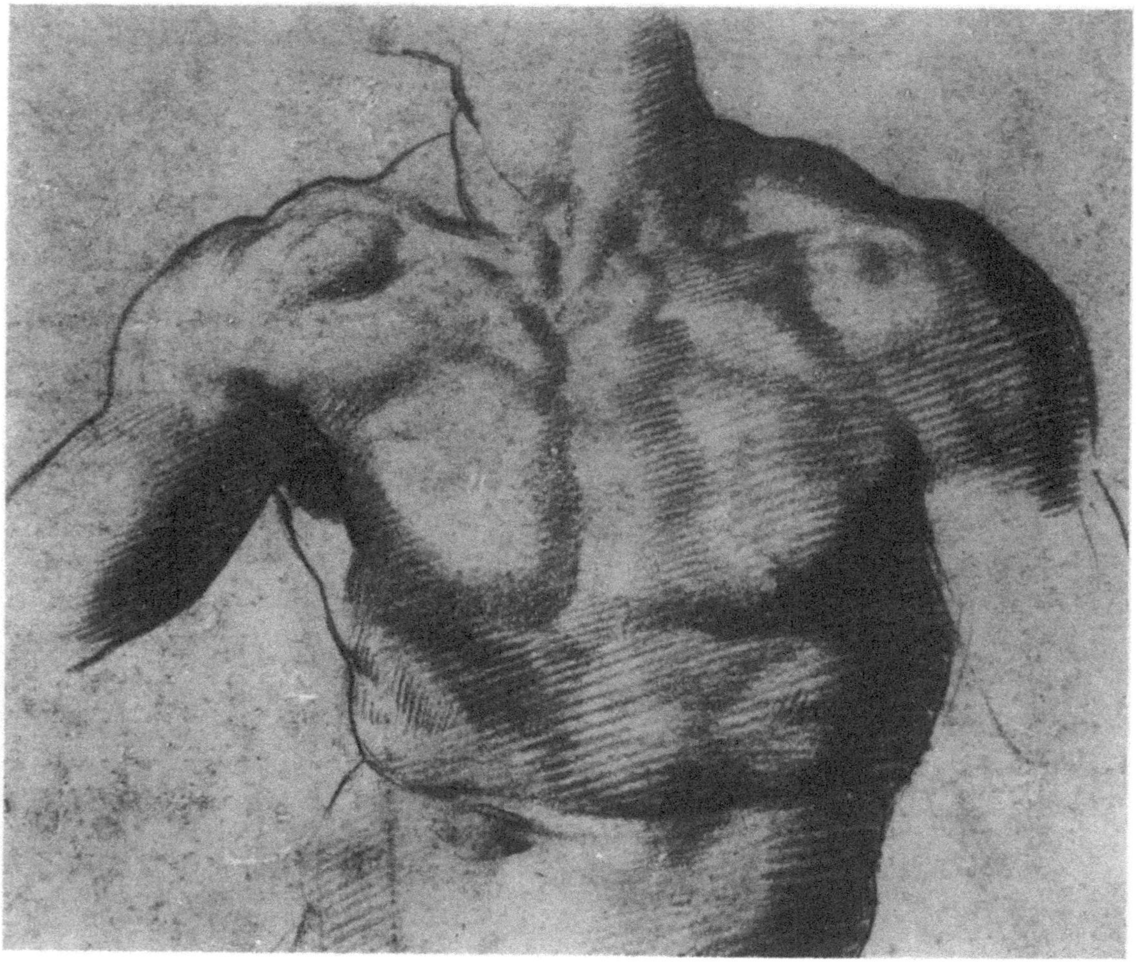

Rosso Fiorentino (Giambattista Rossi; 1494–1541). Study for a male torso; a head for the same figure. Sanguine. Pierpont Morgan Library, New York.

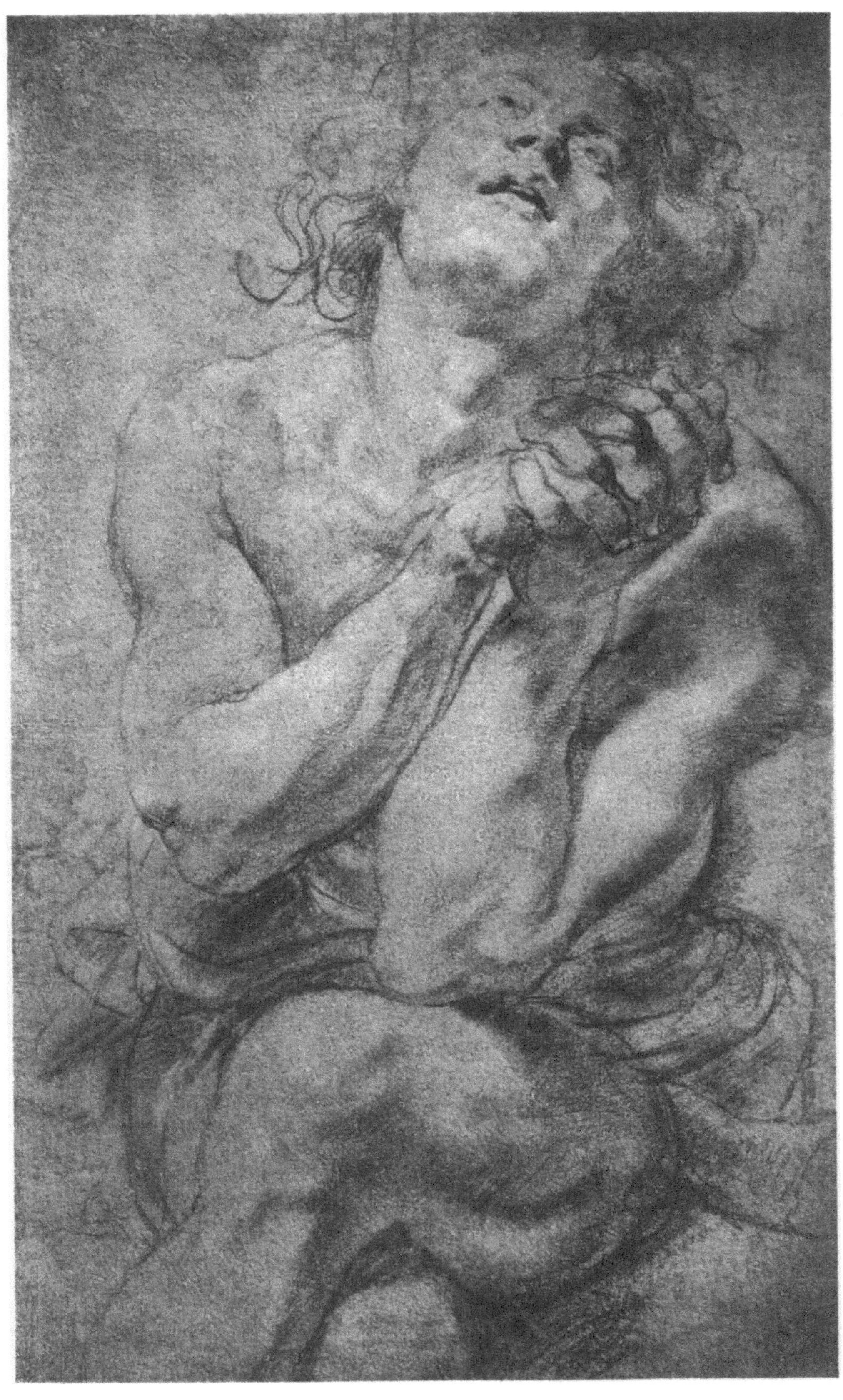

Peter Paul Rubens (1577–1640). A study for *Daniel in the Lions' Den* (National Gallery, Washington). Black chalk.

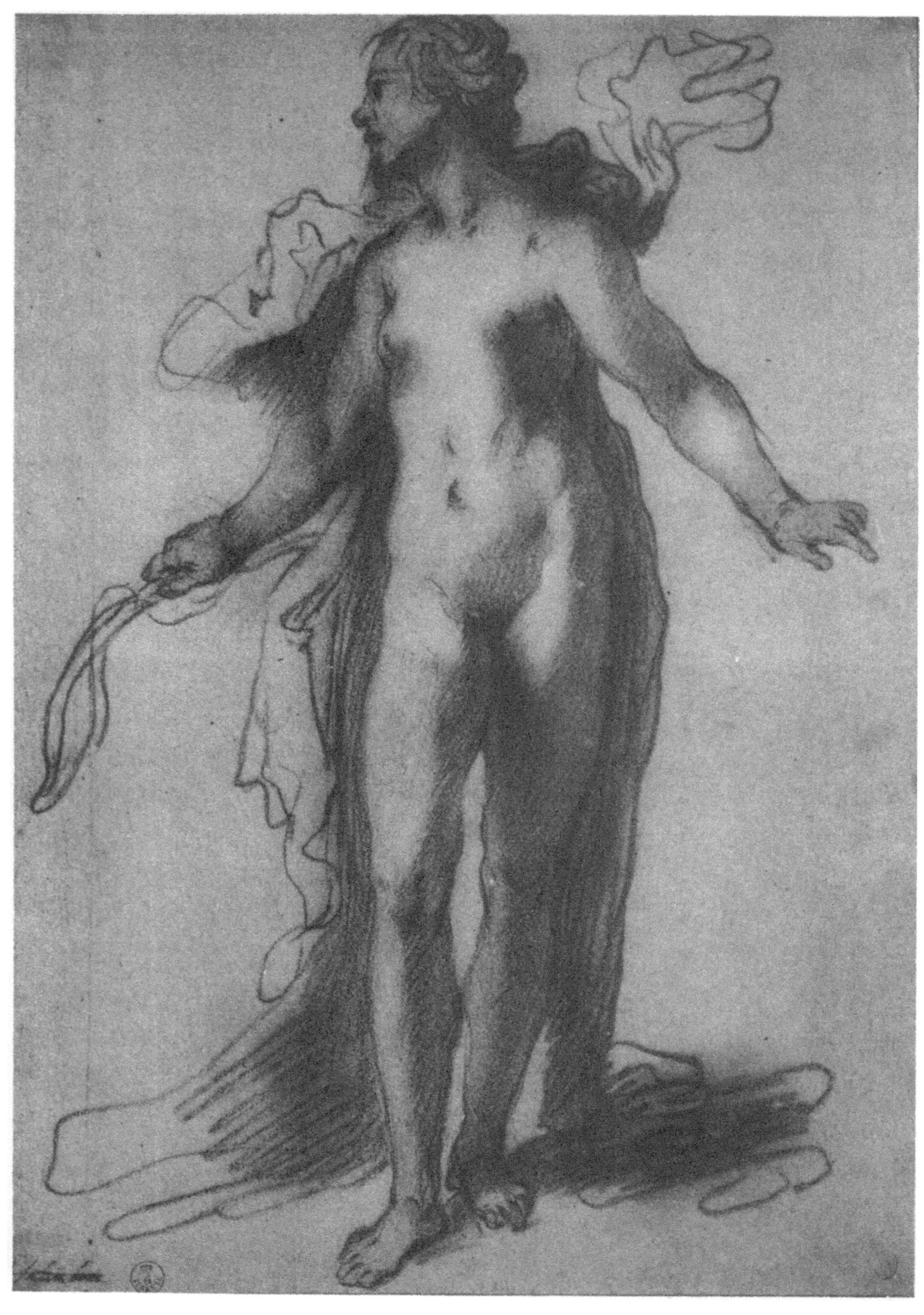

Ventura Salimbeni (1568–1613). Female nude. Sanguine; 330 × 230 mm. Uffizi Gallery, Florence.

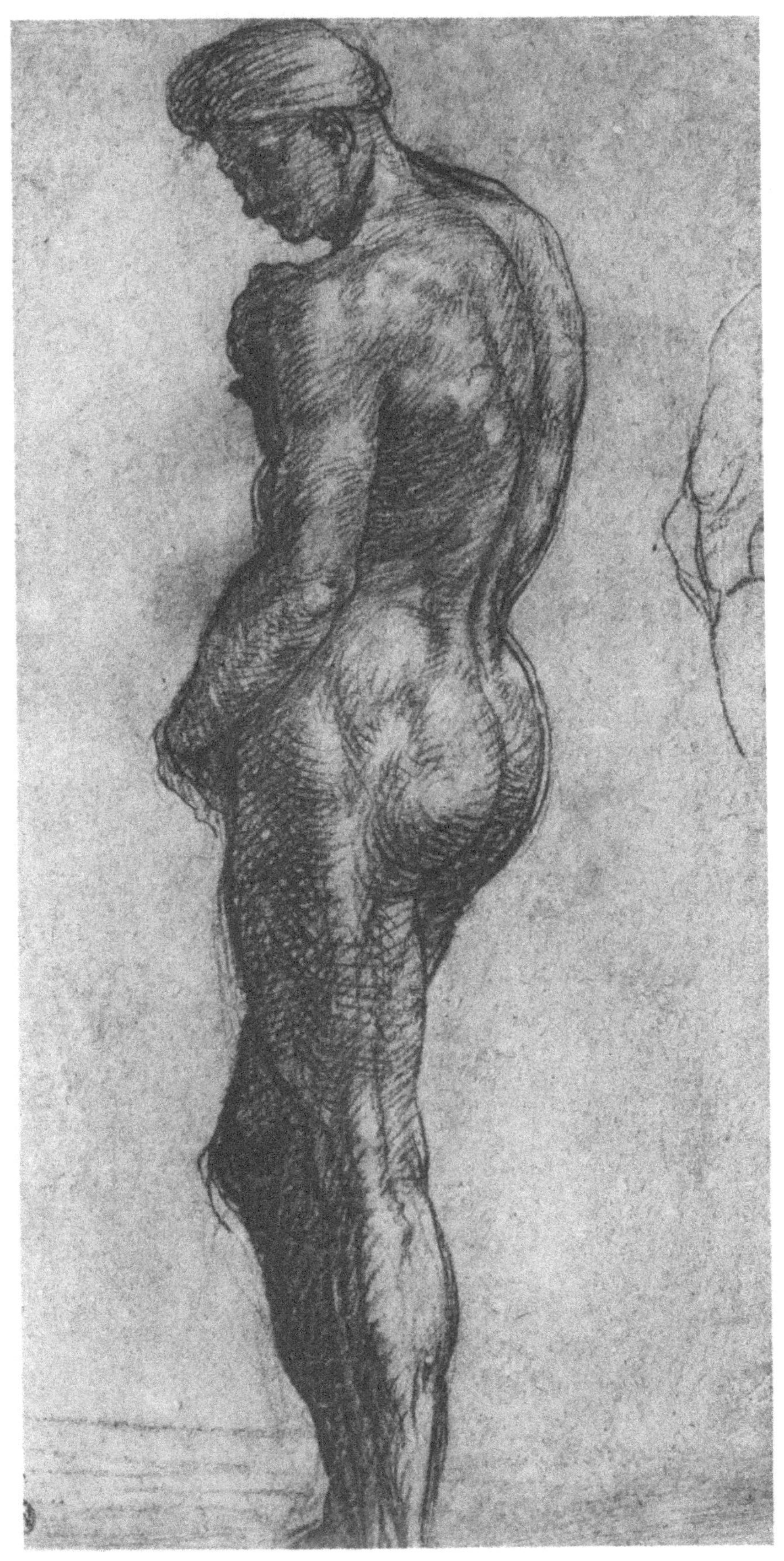

Andrea del Sarto (1487–1530/31). Study of a young man. Sanguine; 395 × 200 mm. Louvre. Paris.

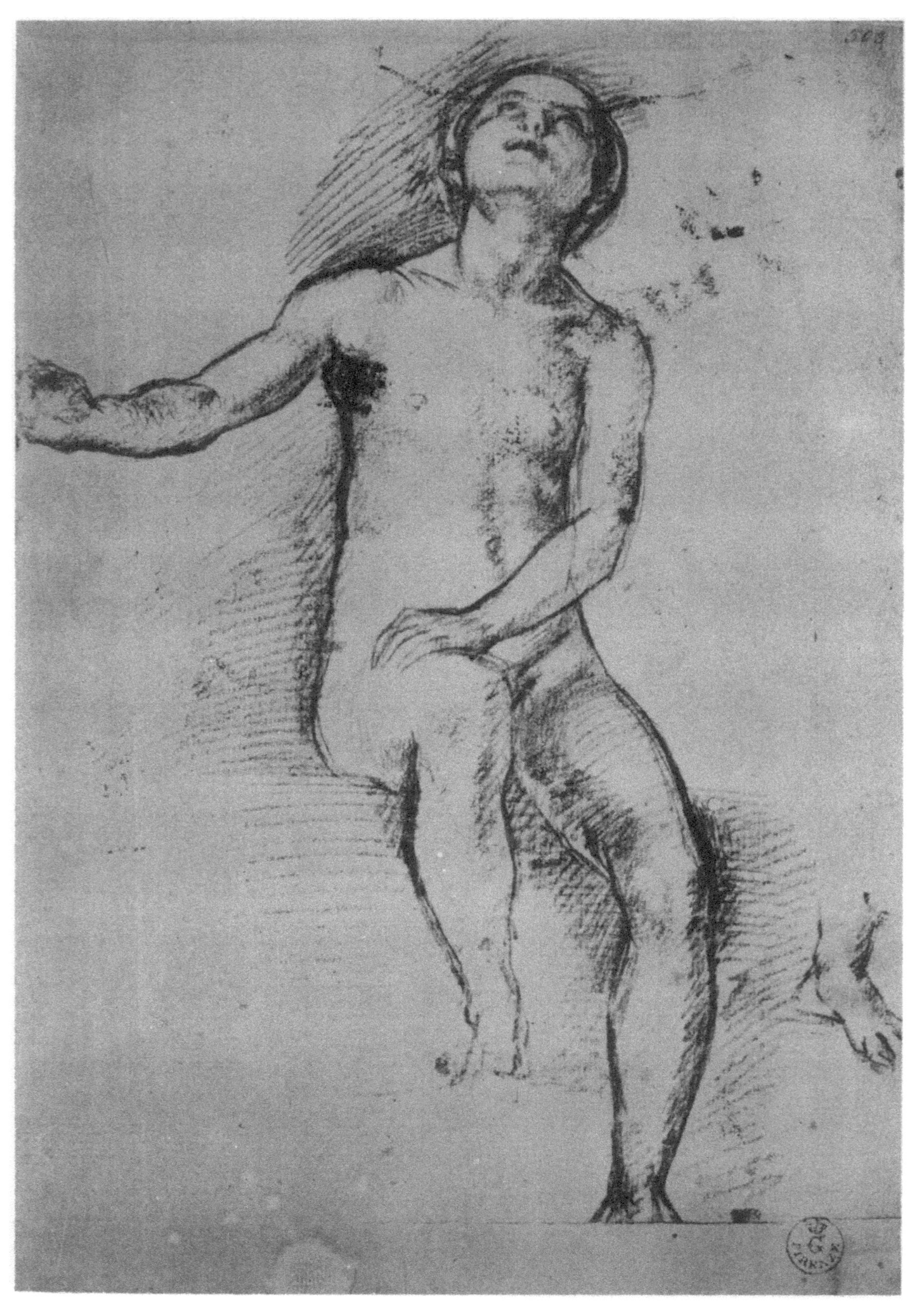

Andrea del Sarto. Female figure. Black chalk on white paper; 260 × 190 mm. Uffizi Gallery, Florence.

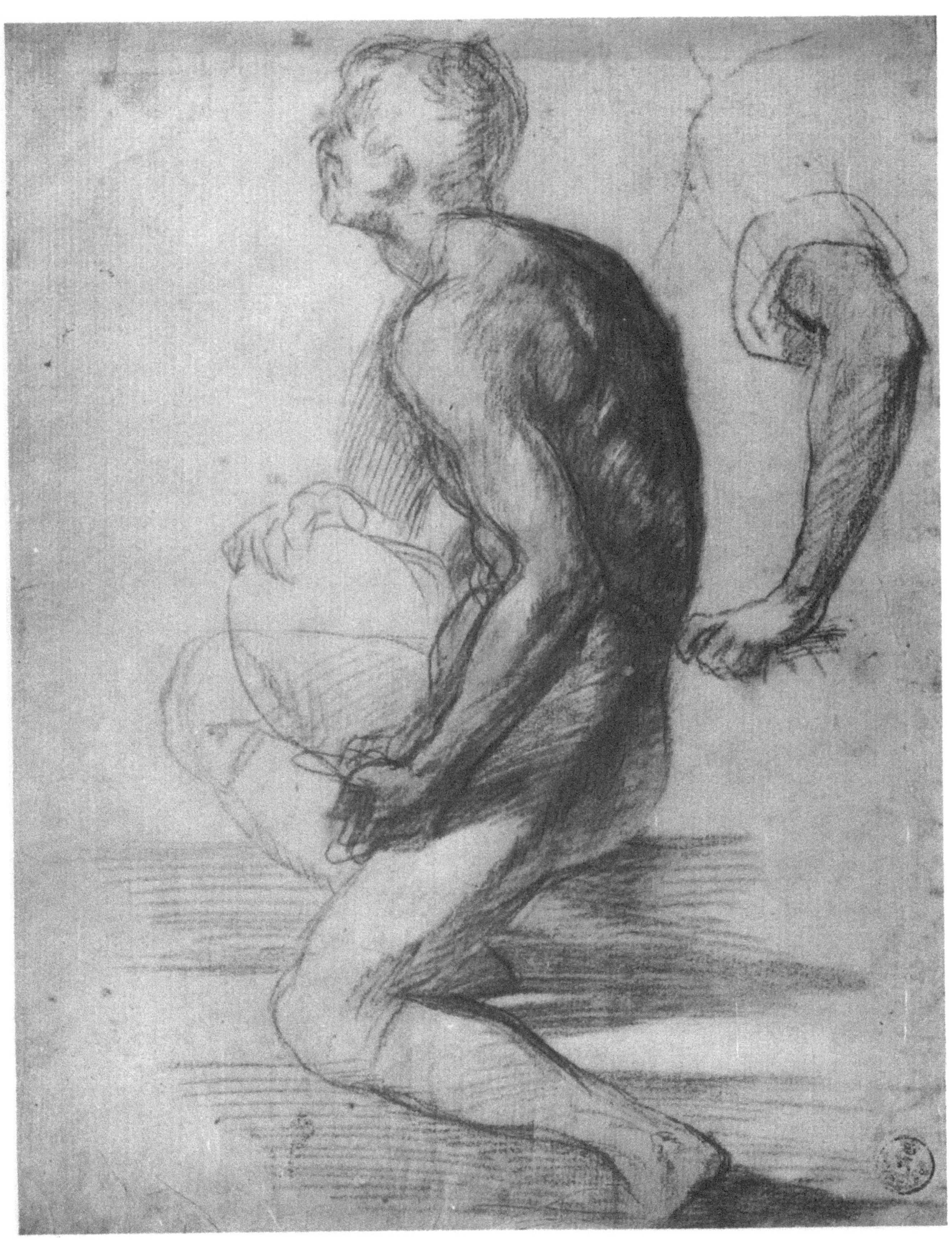

Andrea del Sarto. Male figure. Sanguine on red paper; 265 × 200 mm. Uffizi Gallery, Florence.

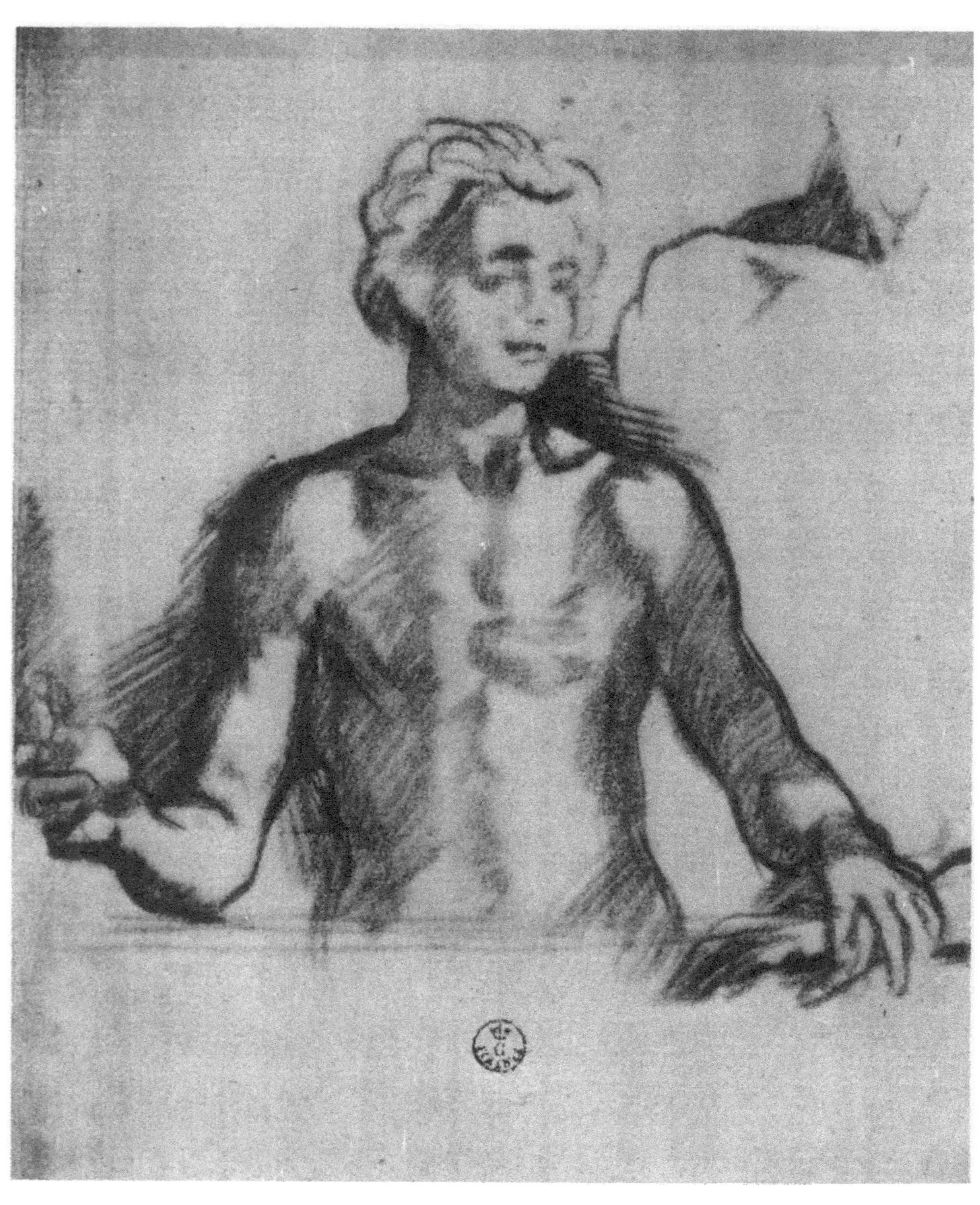

Andrea del Sarto. Male half-figure. Sanguine on white paper; 190 × 150 mm. Uffizi Gallery, Florence.

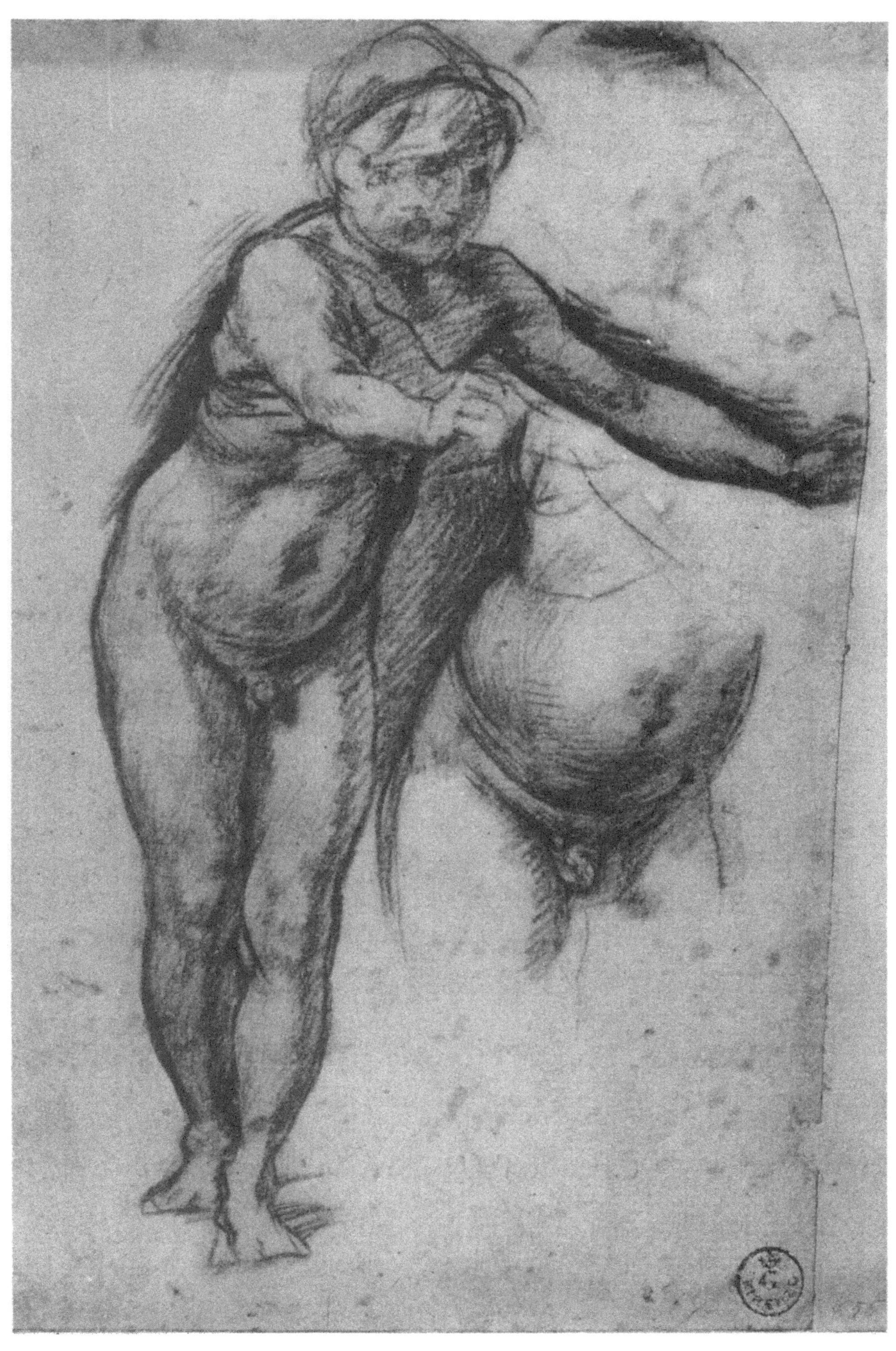

Andrea del Sarto. Study of a child. Sanguine on white paper; 250 × 165 mm. Uffizi Gallery, Florence.

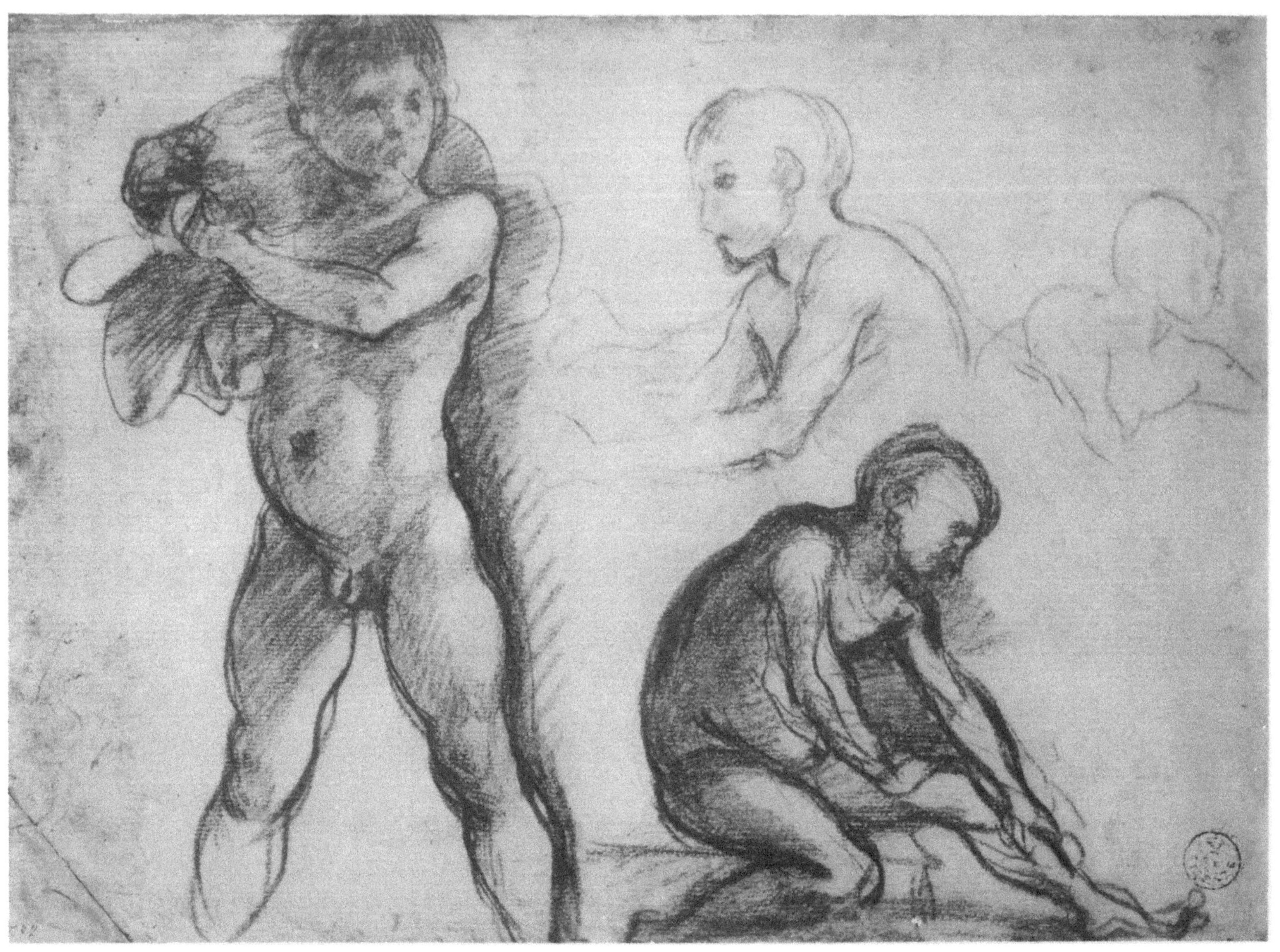

Andrea del Sarto. Studies of children. Sanguine on white paper; 200 × 275 mm. Uffizi Gallery, Florence.

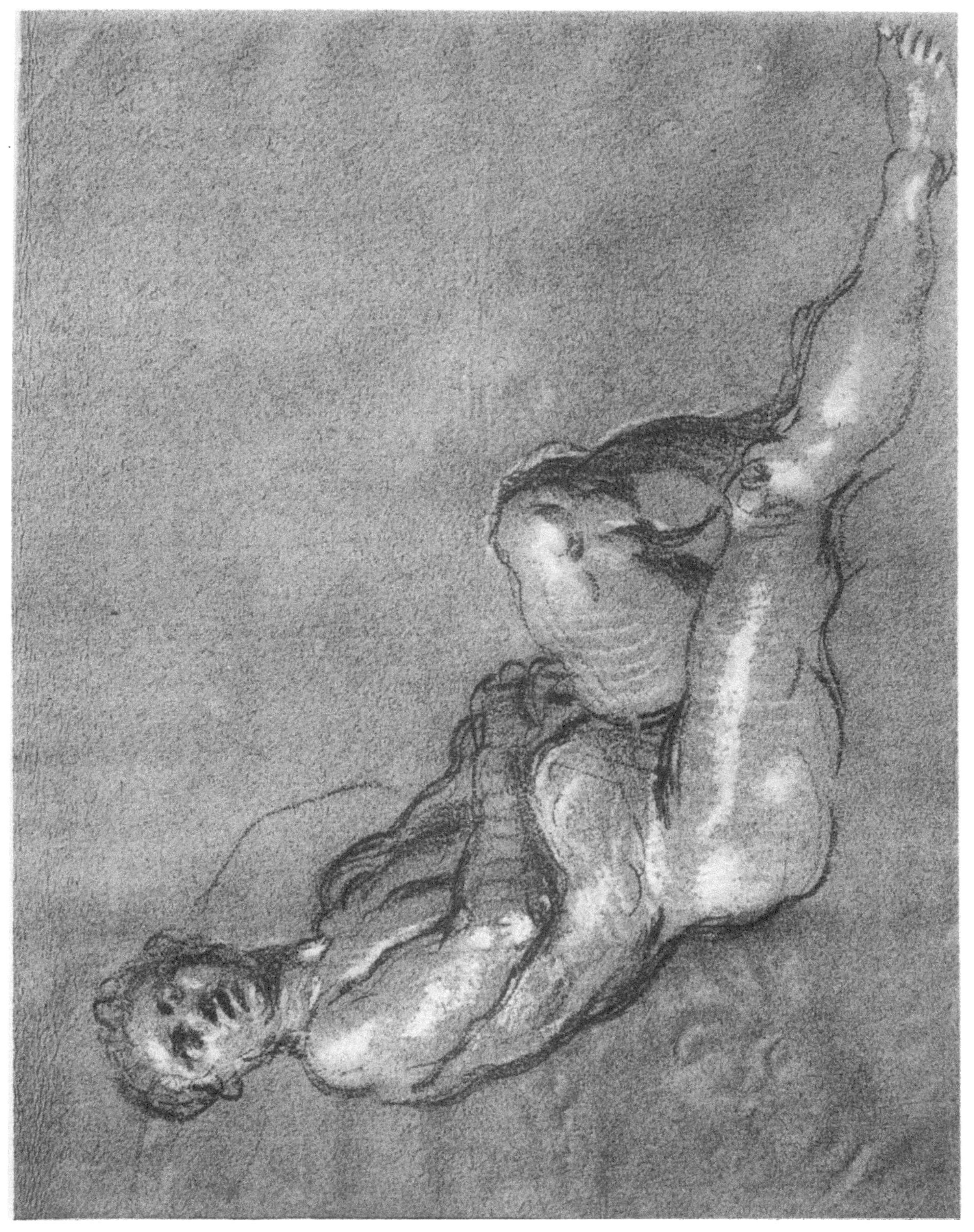

Tintoretto (Jacopo Robusti; 1518/19–1594). Study of a nude man. Chalk on blue paper; 274 × 353 mm. Palazzo Corsini, Rome.

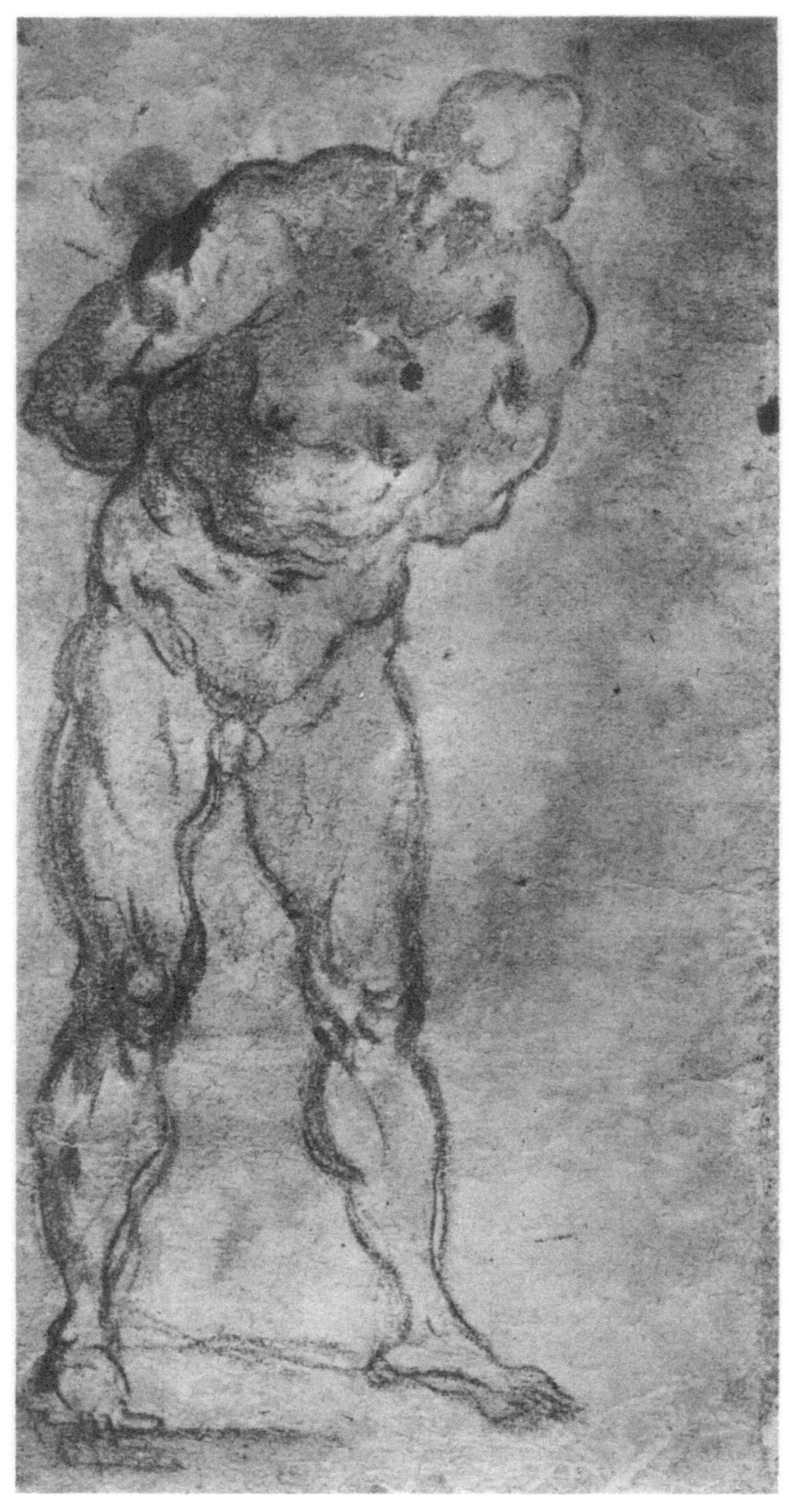

Tintoretto. Study of a nude man for one of the thieves in *Christ Bearing the Cross* (Scuola di San Rocco, Venice). Charcoal on greenish-gray paper; 378 × 201 mm. Uffizi Gallery, Florence.

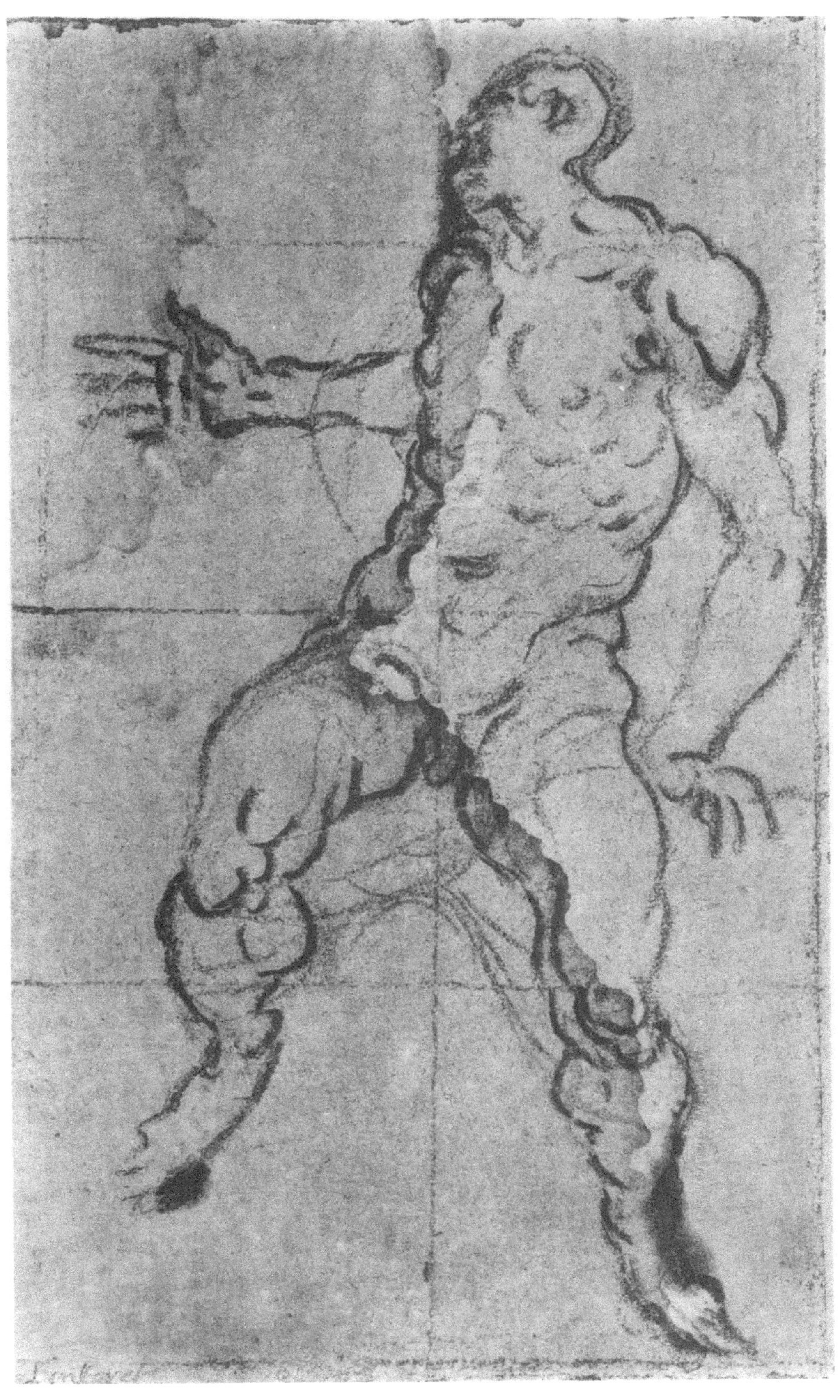

Tintoretto. Study of a nude man. Charcoal on blue paper; 242 × 142 mm.
Landesmuseum, Darmstadt.

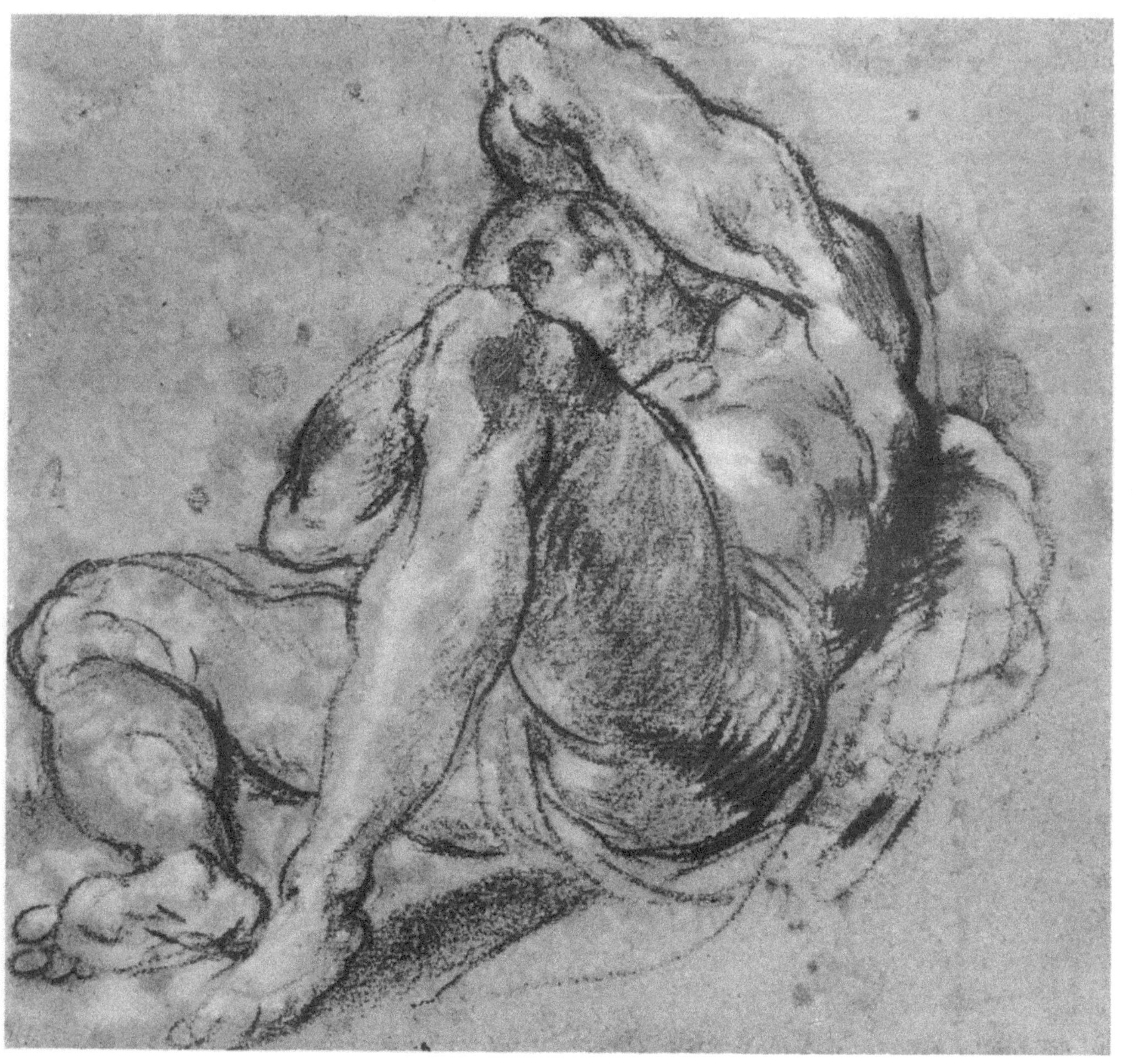

Tintoretto. Study of a nude man. Chalk on gold-brown paper; 210 × 227 mm. Uffizi Gallery, Florence.

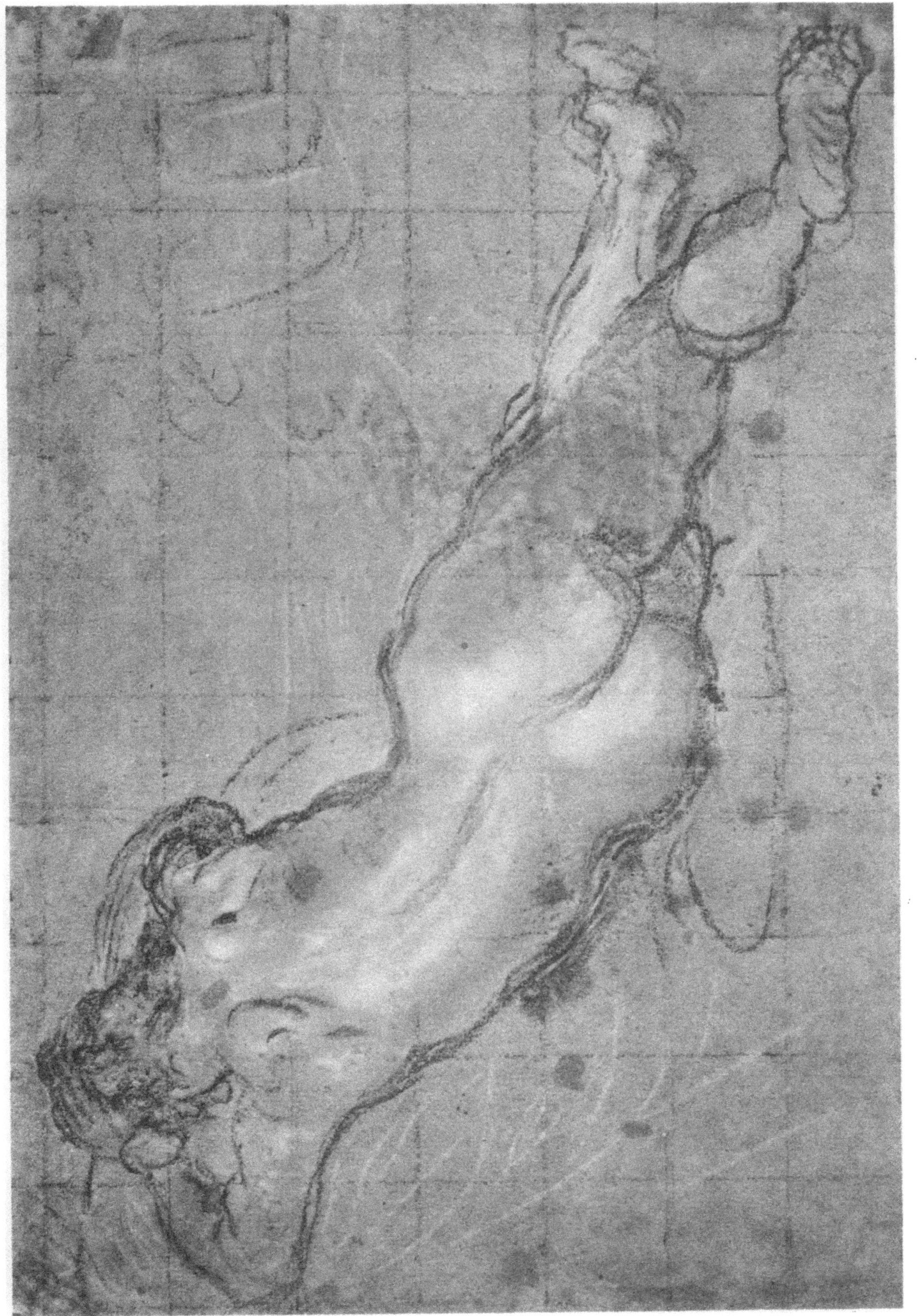

Tintoretto. Study of a nude woman. Charcoal with white heightening on bluish paper; 255 × 380 mm. Uffizi Gallery, Florence.

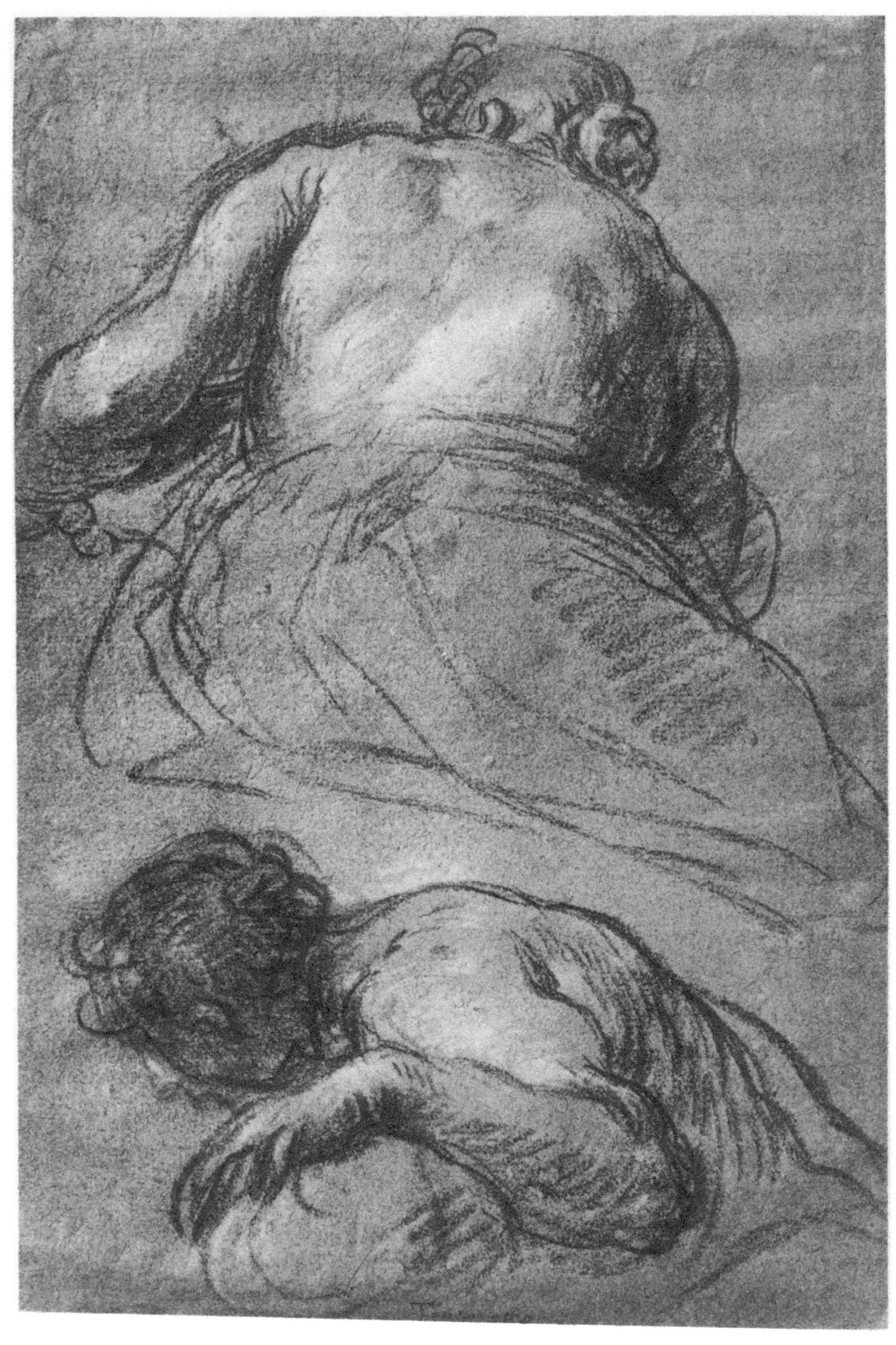

Tintoretto. Two studies of a partially nude woman. Chalk on blue paper; 243 × 161 mm. Palazzo Corsini, Rome.

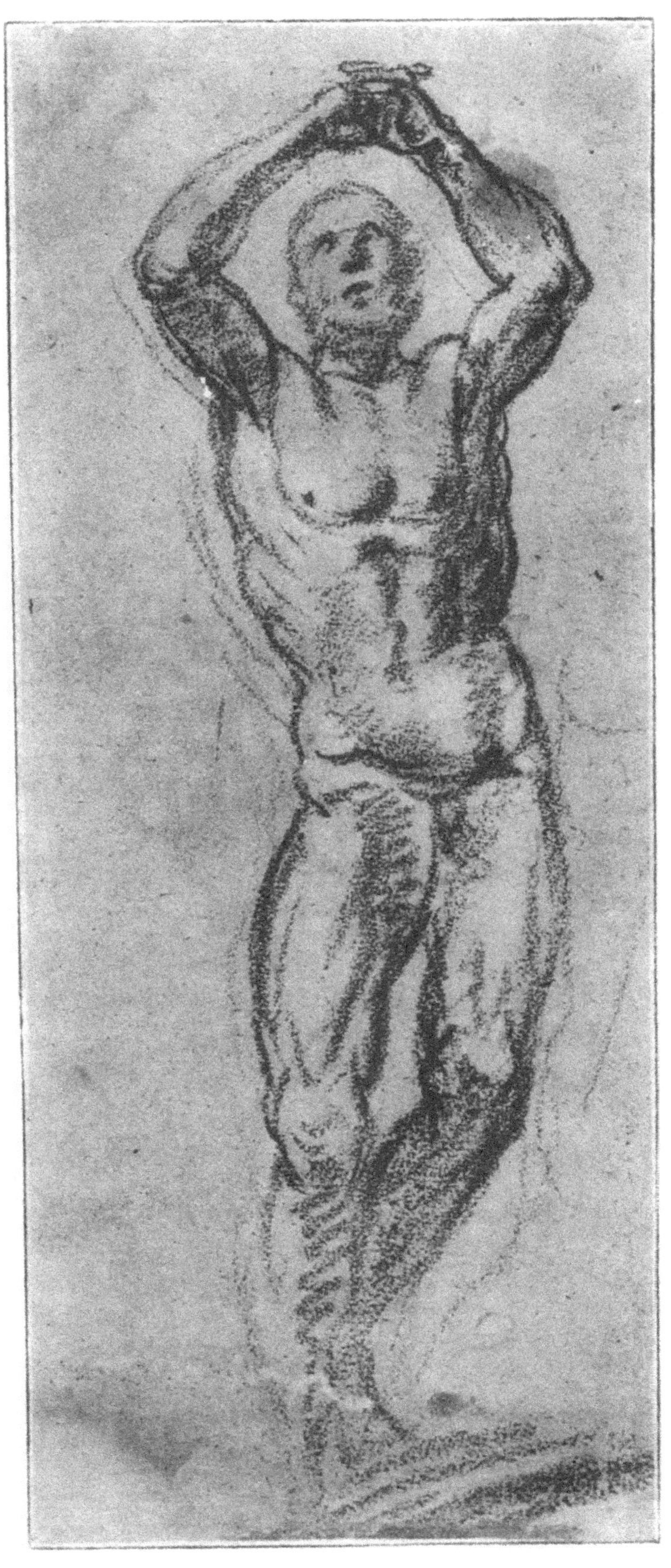

Tintoretto. Study of a nude man. Charcoal on brown paper; 311 × 121 mm. University of Würzburg.

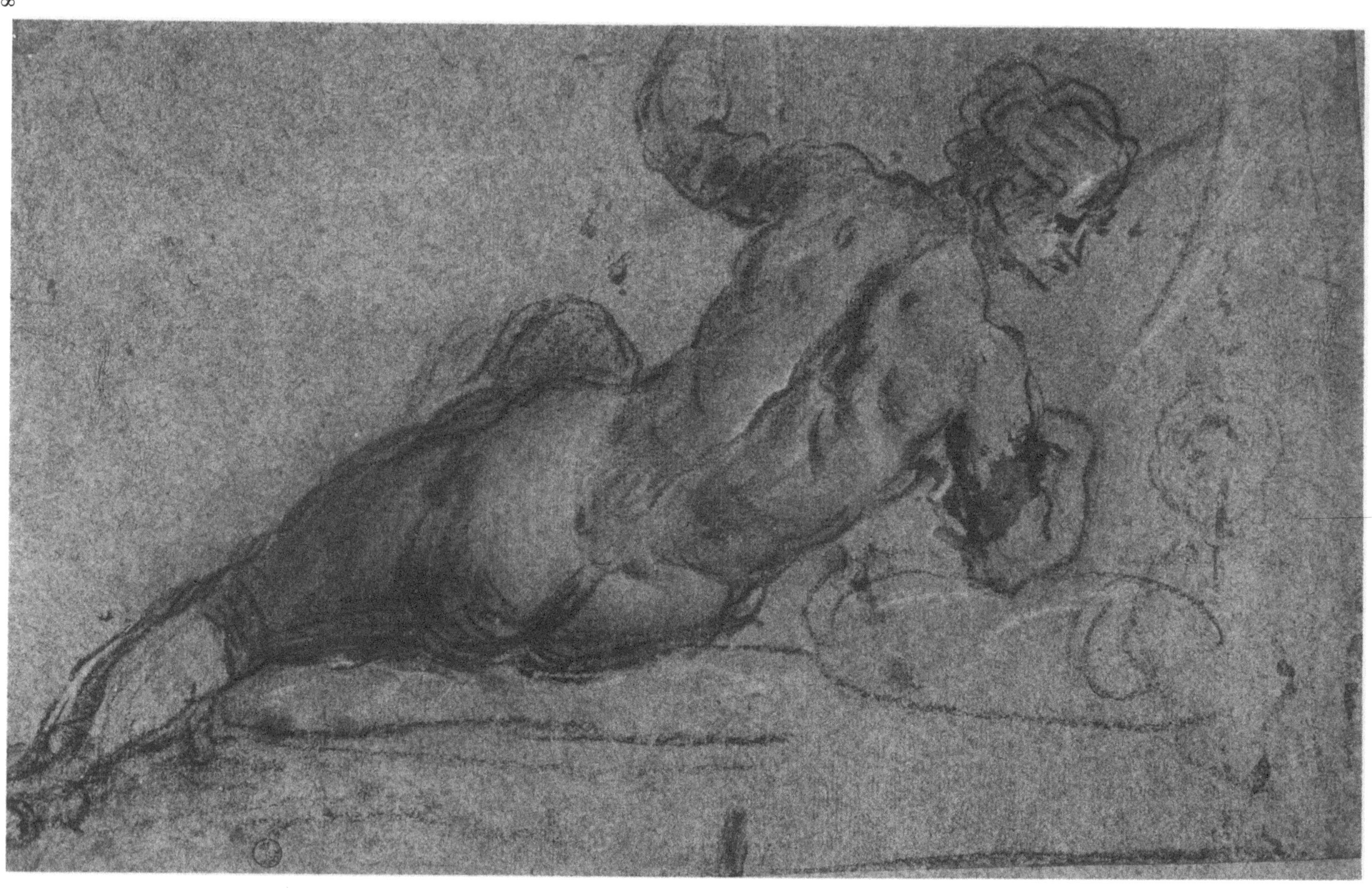

Tintoretto. Reclining female nude. Black crayon and chalk on blue paper; 260 × 420 mm. Uffizi Gallery, Florence.

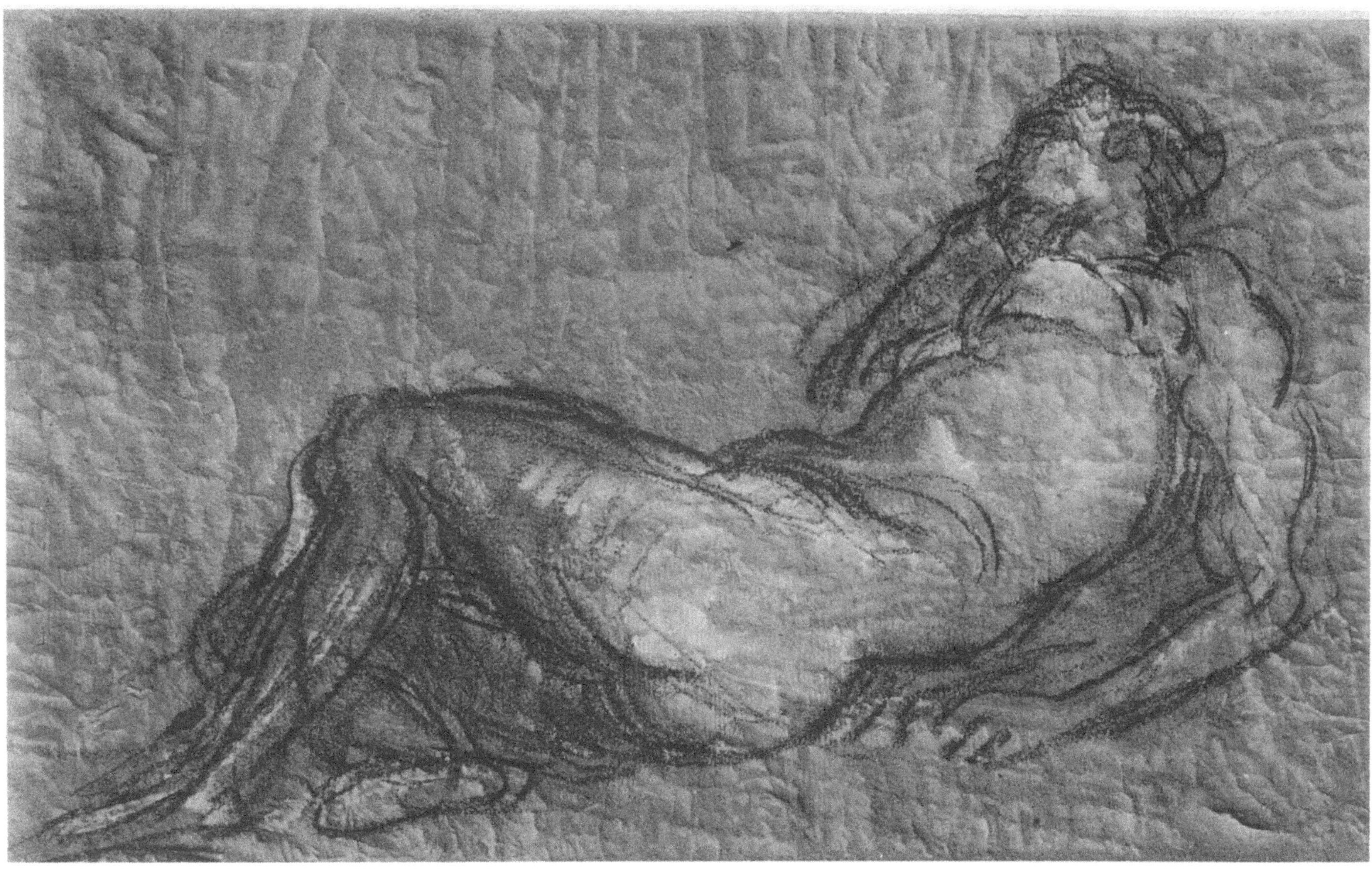

School of Tintoretto. Study of a female nude. Charcoal on gray paper; 220 × 362 mm. Palazzo Corsini, Rome.

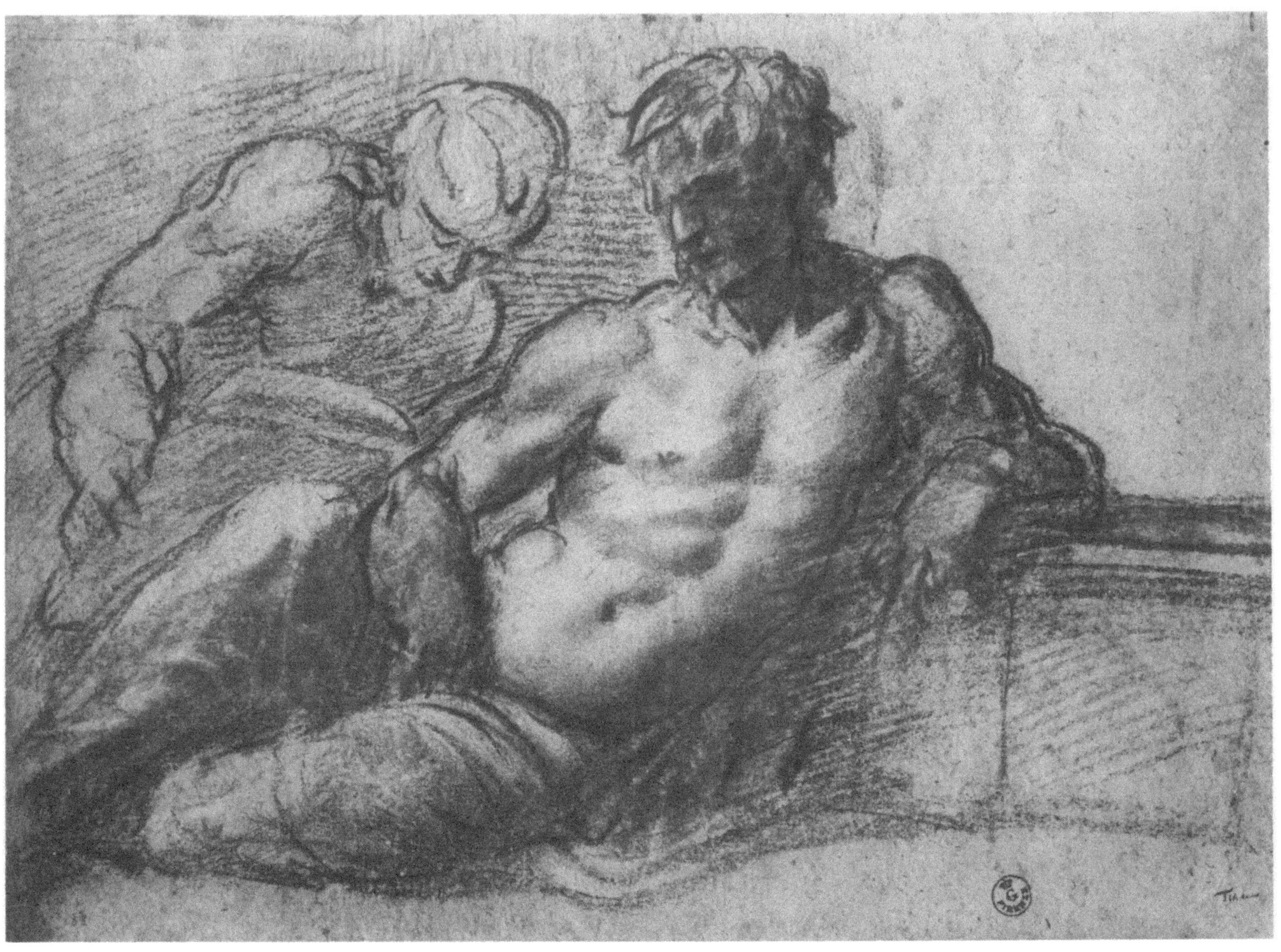

Titian (Tiziano Vecellio; ca. 1485 or 1488/89–1576). Reclining male figure. Charcoal and chalk on blue paper; 280 × 415 mm. Uffizi Gallery, Florence.

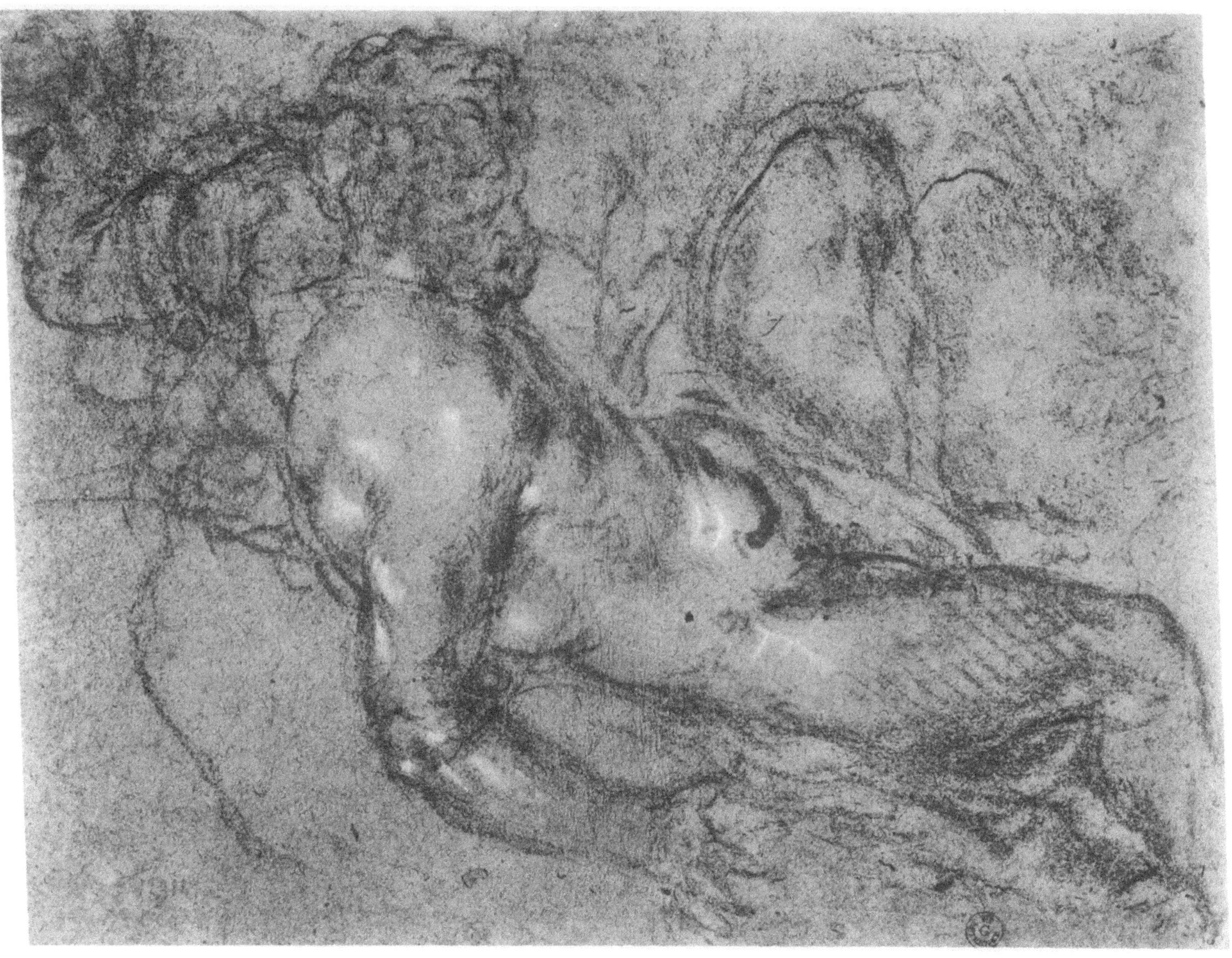

Titian. Reclining male figure. Chalk heightened with white on blue paper; 293 × 400 mm. Uffizi Gallery, Florence.

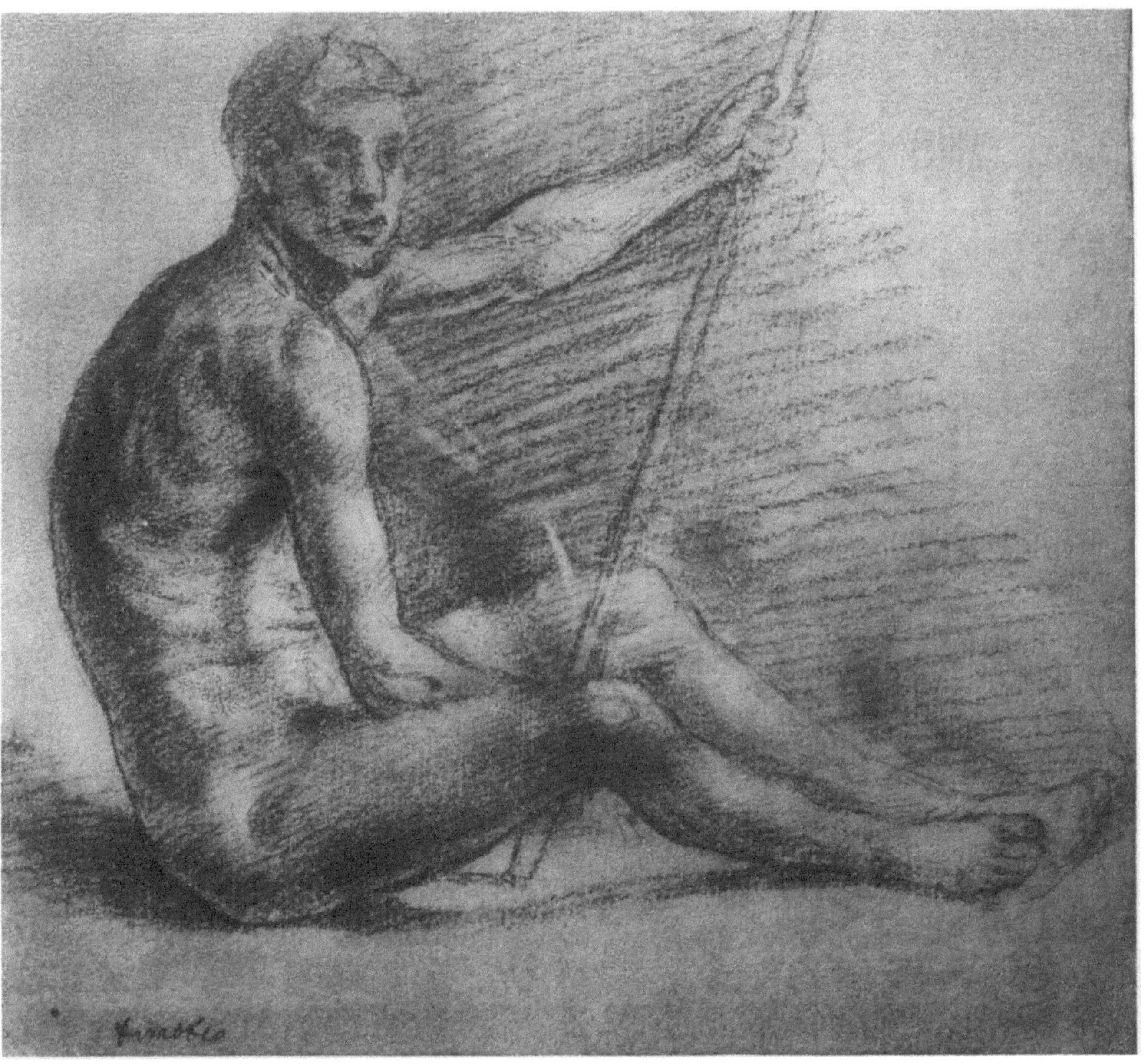

Timoteo delle Vite (1469–1523). Seated man. Black chalk.

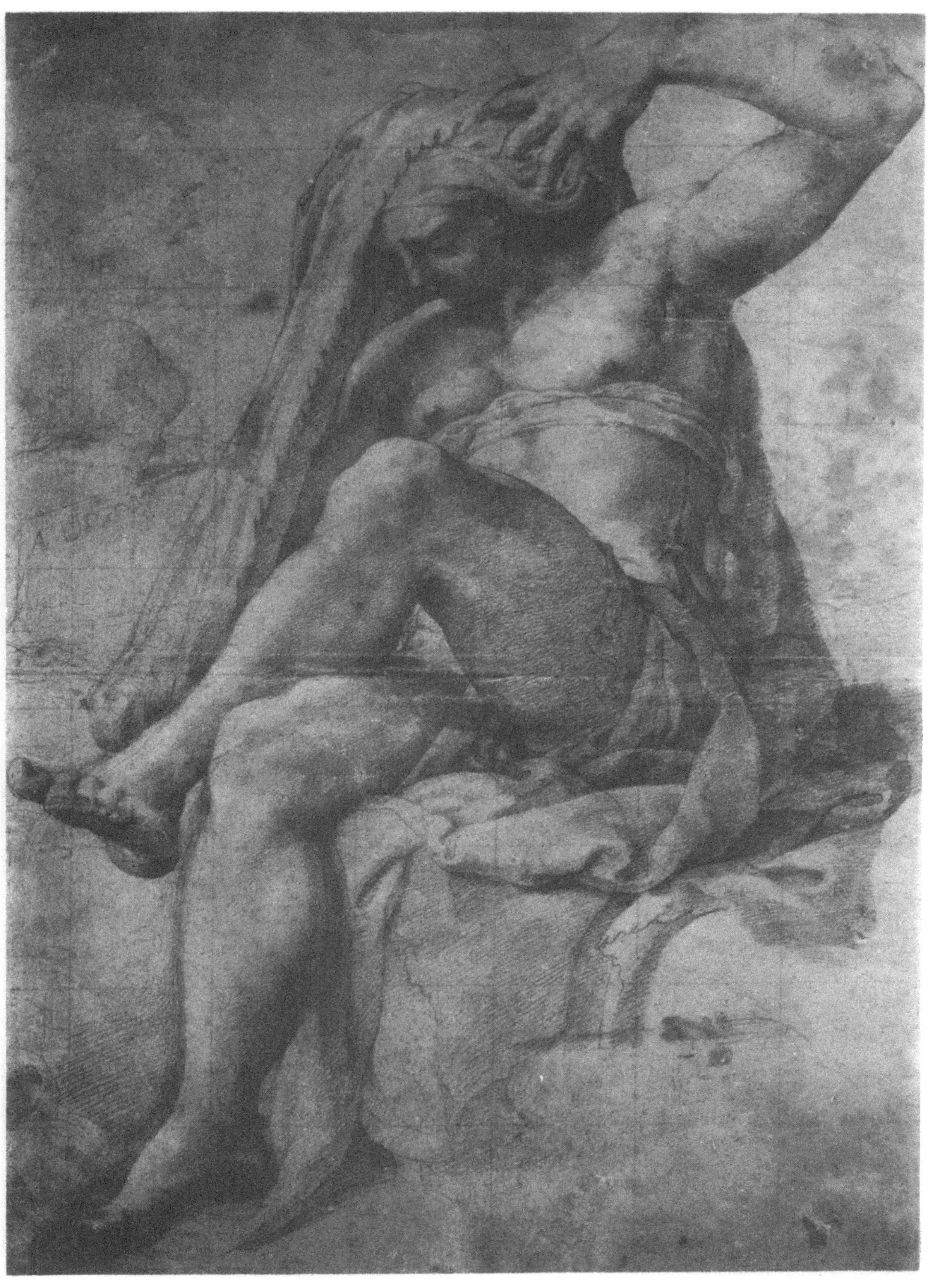

Daniele da Volterra (1509–1566). Study for a sibyl. Sanguine. Pierpont Morgan Library, New York.